William Mackergo Taylor

The Gospel Miracles in their Relation to Christ and Christianity

William Mackergo Taylor

The Gospel Miracles in their Relation to Christ and Christianity

ISBN/EAN: 9783743395077

Manufactured in Europe, USA, Canada, Australia, Japa

Cover: Foto ©Lupo / pixelio.de

Manufactured and distributed by brebook publishing software (www.brebook.com)

William Mackergo Taylor

The Gospel Miracles in their Relation to Christ and Christianity

THE GOSPEL MIRACLES

IN THEIR RELATION

TO

CHRIST AND CHRISTIANITY.

BY

WM. M. TAYLOR, D.D.,

Pastor of the Broadway Tabernacle Church, New York.

NEW YORK:
ANSON D. F. RANDOLPH & COMPANY,
900 BROADWAY, COR. 20th STREET.

NEW YORK:
EDWARD O. JENKINS, PRINTER,
20 *North William St.*

TO

THE MEMBERS OF THE FACULTY

OF

PRINCETON THEOLOGICAL SEMINARY,

WHO

HONORED ME WITH THE APPOINTMENT TO DELIVER THESE LECTURES
ON THE L. P. STONE FOUNDATION, AND AT WHOSE REQUEST
THEY ARE NOW PUBLISHED,

This Volume

IS AFFECTIONATELY INSCRIBED.

April 15, 1880.   WM. M. TAYLOR.

CONTENTS.

LECTURE I.
THE NATURE AND POSSIBILITY OF MIRACLES, . . 1

LECTURE II.
THE SUPERNATURAL IN CHRIST, ... 27

LECTURE III.
THE CREDIBILITY OF MIRACLES, ... 59

LECTURE IV.
THE TESTIMONY IN BEHALF OF MIRACLES, . . 99

LECTURE V.
THE MYTHICAL THEORY, ... 137

LECTURE VI.
THE EVIDENTIAL VALUE OF THE MIRACLES, . . 171

LECTURE VII.
THE SPIRITUAL SIGNIFICANCE OF THE MIRACLES, . 205

APPENDIX, ... 231

THE NATURE
AND POSSIBILITY OF MIRACLES.

LECTURE I.
THE NATURE AND POSSIBILITY OF MIRACLES.

Acts ii. 22: Jesus of Nazareth, a man approved of God among you by miracles and wonders; signs, which God did by him, in the midst of you.

IN entering on the subject which is to occupy our attention throughout these lectures, it is needful that we should have a clear idea of the place which an inquiry into the credibility and evidential value of miracles has in the investigation of the nature and origin of Christianity. These are not the first topics that challenge consideration in the examination of the Scriptures; nor are they dependent for their right adjustment on our acceptance of the doctrine that the Evangelists and Apostles were divinely inspired. It is often alleged, however, that the defenders of the faith are guilty of disingenuousness, inasmuch as, at one time, they use the inspiration and authority of Scripture for the purpose of proving the reality of the miracles; while at another, they employ the reality of the miracles for the purpose of establishing the inspired authority of the Scriptures. But a little attention to the logical order in which the different subjects connected with the Bible present themselves for examination, will convince any one that such an accusation is unjust. For, taking up these ancient books, just as we would any other productions, the first question which arises is, by whom were they written? the next, have they come to us as their authors wrote them? the next, at what date were they composed? Then having satisfactorily disposed of these matters, we are met with the inquiry, are they credible records of actual occurrences? and it is at this point that the whole debate over the miracles arises. On the one hand, it is alleged that the very presence of the record of such things in the gospels gives a legendary character to them, and imposes a heavy burden on their credibility, or relegates them to the category of myths; and, on the other, it is contended that, though they be works out of the usual experience of men, their performance by such an one as Jesus is described to have been, is perfectly in harmony with everything else that is said about Him, is well established by testimony of the weightiest sort, and does not at all derogate from the general trustworthiness of the narrative. Here, then, an arrest is put upon our progress, and we have to settle whether these miracles were genuine or not. But, supposing we come to the conclusion that they were genuine, we are then in a position to go forward and ask farther: What do these supernatural works say regarding the person and mission of Him by whom they were performed? In other words, when we are dealing with the credibility of the evangelic narratives, we have to answer the question how far that is affected by the accounts of miracles which they contain; and then, the credibility established, when we come to deal with the divine origin and authority of the Gospel, we have to ask what the miracles say concerning Him who wrought them, and the system in connection with which they were performed? Thus there is no vicious circle, but a strictly logical method is pursued, and each subject of investigation follows naturally on that by which it is preceded.

It will not be expected that I should go back over all those matters of criticism, genuineness, and authenticity to which I have referred. I must be allowed, for the purposes of these discourses, to assume as already proved, that the gospels were written before the end of the first century, that they are the productions of the men whose names they bear, and that they are in our hands substantially as they were when they came from those of their authors.

Now, on a perusal of these four biographies it will be at once apparent, that the miracles which they record can not be eliminated from the history, without virtually destroying its character. From beginning to end the evangelical narrative is homogeneous; and nothing can be taken from it without not merely injuring, but also overthrowing all the rest. Its several parts fit into each other like the stones of an arch, and if one be removed, all the others must ultimately fall. The miraculous birth of Jesus is felt by every reader to correspond with His resurrection from the dead and ascension into glory; while all that lies between is recognized as being in perfect harmony with both. The supernatural—whether rightly or wrongly claimed for it—is its differentiating quality; and if that be taken from it, nothing really distinctive or peculiar remains. Even as a literary production it could not survive the removal from it of its miraculous incidents, for these are so inwrought into its fabric, that any attempt to cut them out would destroy it as effectually as the removal of its pictorial patterns from a piece of tapestry would ruin the entire production. The miracles are the weft, and the discourses and other incidents are the woof of a history whose unity is constituted by the interweaving of the two—and the removal of either is the destruction of the web. Separate threads might remain, but you could have no cloth. If you abstract the miracles you might still be able to keep some parts of the Sermon on the Mount, but you would have overturned the foundation on which that constantly recurring, "I say unto you," rests; and with that would go the very element of authority in it which so impressed those who heard it at the first. You might preserve also some of the parables; but even these taken away from the setting in which they stand and from the interpretation given to them in many cases by the divine personality and history of the speaker, would lose most of their significance and power. You might retain, too, a figure that you still called Jesus of Nazareth, but he would not be the Jesus whom the Evangelists have portrayed, for he would have lost his moral greatness and his distinctive individuality, and would be felt to be no more to us than one of the old Grecian sages. Try it for yourselves. Take the gospel by Matthew, erase from it everything of the supernatural, and what will remain? only a heap of fragments. Instead of a statue, a torso, and even that all battered and broken. Instead of a temple brightened and glorified by the inhabitation of God, a heap of loose stones having no more connection with each other than that which juxtaposition gives them. Whatever else may be said, therefore, this must be admitted, that these Evangelists designed to depict a supernatural life. That which they describe is in itself one great miracle; and if you attempt to eliminate the miraculous from it, you will find that all of it evaporates under your hands.

It has been alleged by many, indeed, that they can dispense with the miracles, and yet obtain all the spiritual good that they require from Jesus Christ. But if those who express that opinion still believe in the Deity of Jesus, they have in the Incarnation the very thing which they repudiate, and they have it, too, in a form which furnishes the explanation of all the other supernatural things which the gospels record. If, again, they disbelieve His deity, their rejection of the miracles carries with it the condemnation of His moral character; for He laid claim to be a miracle-worker, and it remains to be explained by them how one who must have been a deliberate deceiver, has obtained and maintained such a hold upon the hearts of men, and has more than all others contributed to the formation in them of a character that is distinguished for truth and uprightness.

Moreover, it must not be forgotten, that the distinctive doctrines of Christianity are all the formulization of supernatural facts in the history of Christ. The incarnation and resurrection are both miracles, and shorn of these, what is left of the Gospel which we preach? Take that ancient confession of faith, which we call "The Apostles' Creed," and eliminate from it everything that expresses miracle or presupposes it, and see how little would remain. Only the first four words, "I believe in God the Father;" and these also would go if with some modern philosophers we include God under the supernatural. Unless, therefore, we are willing to go back to the barest theism or the darkest atheism, we are committed to the acceptance and defence of the supernatural.

It may be possible for a time for those who have themselves given up their faith in miracles, to retain some of the things which they have absorbed, in spite of their intellectual skepticism, from the evangelical atmosphere in which they have been trained, and in which, largely at least, they still live. But it is none the less true that apart from the supernatural in it, even Christianity becomes the merest theism; with nothing in it of the character of a revelation, and differing only in degree from other systems of men. Admirably has one said, " Some there are, no doubt, who talk of such theistic beliefs, combined with high morality, as the essence of Christianity, but with what right? Theism and morality, however essential to Christianity, are common in greater or less degree to many other systems also; while all that is distinctive in Christian theism and morality comes from the relation in which these elements stand to the historical facts of its founder's life and work. To call these common elements, then, the essence of Christianity—ignoring all that, whether by ennobling them, or still more by its own proper significance and worth, distinguishes Christianity from other religions—is not only to sin against the unanimous witness of the Christian Church throughout all ages (which must surely be admitted as decisive), but is intrinsically unfair."* This, therefore, is no mere mat-

---

* George Warrington. " Can we Believe in Miracles?" pp. 5. 6.

ter of secondary importance. The debate about the supernatural is no skirmish between stragglers on the outskirts of the field: it is a conflict for the very center and key of the position, and no Christian can be indifferent to its issue. "It is not a vain thing for us, because it is our life."

Let us, then, with a full realization of all that is involved in the case, proceed to an investigation of the subject.

And first, let us endeavor to obtain a correct idea of what a miracle is. In the New Testament four words are employed to designate supernatural works, namely, miracles, wonders, signs, and works. The first ($δυνάμεις$) signifies "powers," and refers to the agency by which they were produced; the second ($τέρατα$) denotes "marvels," and describes their effect on the minds of the beholders; the third ($σημεία$), "signs," has special reference to their significance in connection with the system by whose inaugurator they were wrought; while the last ($έργα$), "works," is used only by Jesus himself, and is in His lips, as we shall see later on, peculiarly suggestive, since it implies that the effects which seemed to others, and rightly seemed to them, so marvellous, were from His own point of view perfectly natural, as being, in fact, only the manifestation of His Deity.

A miracle we define to be a work out of the usual sequence of secondary causes and effects, which can not be accounted for by the ordinary action of these causes, and which is produced by the agency of God in connection with the word of one who claims to be His representative. It is not a violation of what are popularly called the "laws of nature," and I can not but regard it as unfortunate that any such description of it should ever have been given. If from the operation of precisely the same secondary causes, an entirely opposite effect were to be produced, that would be a violation of a law of nature. But a miracle is not such an effect; it is a work which is due wholly to the introduction and operation of a new cause. When a boy throws a stone up into the air there is a counteraction of the force of gravity, so far as the stone is concerned, but there is no violation of the law of gravitation, for the simple explanation is, that another force, generated in the will, and exerted by the muscular energy of the boy, has come into operation and performed its work, while the force of gravity is really as strong as it ever was. In like manner, a miracle does not violate nature; but a new force comes in at the moment to produce a supernatural effect.

Neither can a miracle truthfully be described as the suspension of a law of nature; for using the analogy which I have just employed, even while the stone was ascending into the air, the force of gravity continued, and the law of gravitation remained the principle on which the material universe is regulated. A suspension of any law throughout the universe, even for the briefest time, would issue in the most disastrous results. But a miracle is not such a suspension. It is the production of a new effect, by the intervention of a new cause, which brings about, not the abrogation of any law, but only a deviation, in a single instance, from that which is the ordinary course of things. There needs, therefore, be no jealousy of miracles on the part of those whose office it is to investigate the operation of the forces of that which they call nature. There could be no exceptional deviations, if there were no uniformity as a rule; and so it is as essential to the advocates of the supernatural, as it is to the disciples of science, to contend for the regularity and constancy, or, to use the strongest word, the uniformity of the course of nature.

But, it is objected, that the laws of nature are absolutely rigid in their uniformity, and that such a deviation from that as a miracle involves is a pure impossibility. This is the ground taken up by many in these days, and therefore it must be well examined, if we would dislodge them from its occupancy. Let it be conceded, then, that speaking of the physical universe alone, this absolute constancy in the sequence of antecedents and consequents is not only an irrefutable inference from the observation of

NATURE AND POSSIBILITY OF MIRACLES. 13

phenomena, but also an indispensable requisite to the training of man as a moral being. We fully endorse here the words of an eloquent writer: "Without a reliable universe no moral character could grow. A fickle world admits only of a lawless race, and no obedience could be required from those who are planted among shifting conditions, to whom foresight is denied, and whose wisdom is as likely to go astray as their folly. All human habits are formed by a mutual understanding between man and nature."* So the constancy, or, if you will, the uniformity of the operations of nature, is a truth which is of as much importance to the Christian moralist as it is to the physical philosopher. It is not only a truth which must be accepted, but it is also an indispensable factor in the formation of character.

But when we speak of the uniformity of the operations of the laws of nature, what precisely do we mean by "laws" and what by "nature"? The questions are important, because of the different senses in which the words are used among us, and the consequent liability to which we are exposed of giving to them a meaning in one connection which is correct only in another. As regards "law," the Duke of Argyll in his admirable volume on "The Reign of

---

* Rev. James Martineau, D.D., "Hours of Thought on Sacred Things," p. 77.

Law," has enumerated no fewer than five distinct senses in which it is used by good and reputable writers; but, for the present, it will be enough to distinguish between the two which are most commonly confounded. In its physical sense, a law is an invariable sequence of antecedents and consequents. We see that certain things invariably follow certain other things, and we generalize our observation into something which we call the law of the phenomena. In this sense a law is a human inference from the observation of the operations of nature; and as Sir John Herschel long ago remarked, "the use of the word in this connection has relation to us as understanding rather than to the universe as obeying certain rules."* Thus understood, it must be evident to every one that a law can be the cause of nothing. The law of gravitation does not make any body fall to the earth or hold any planet in its course; it is only the name which men have given to the formula which they have deduced from their observation of falling bodies and of the solar system. It is itself the result of the classification of human observations, and can not therefore be metamorphosed into the cause which produces the phenomena that have been thus observed and classified. We distinguish here between law and force. Force

---

* Sir John Herschel, "Preliminary Discourse on Astronomy."

is the energy which produces the effects; but law is the observed manner in which force works in the production of these effects. So far all is clear. But then, in the moral sphere, the term "law" is used to denote a rule of conduct which we are bound to obey; and thus it has come about that, almost insensibly to themselves, many have imported this idea of obligation from the moral into the physical sphere, and look upon a law of nature as enforcing the sequences of which it is really only the record written in the short-hand of a convenient formula. We must be on our guard, therefore, against introducing the element of causation into our conception of a law of nature. Such a law causes nothing. Force is the active energy; law is the observed manner in which force works. But now, supposing that force to be, in the last resort, the volition or power of a personal omnipotent being, where is the impossibility of its being put forth, in exceptional instances, and for a sufficient purpose, in a way different from that in which it is usually exerted? If law may be regarded as the observed manner in which God has ordinarily chosen to carry on the operations of the physical universe, is it not just as possible for Him to vary that order in exceptional cases, and for a specific and worthy purpose, as it is to maintain it in uniformity? If nature be God's usual action, is there any impossibility involved in the conception of miracle as unusual Divine action?* or must we regard these so-called laws as chains wherewith the Deity has bound Himself, and by which He is held from doing anything, no matter for what purpose, different from what He has always been observed by men to do?

The force of these considerations is increased when we ask further, what is that "nature" of which we speak when we use the phrase the "laws of nature"? If it be restricted to merely physical phenomena, then it must be confessed that we have in them no experience or observation of any interference with the uniformity of its operations; but if, within the domain of nature, we include human nature, then we can no longer make any such admission. For here we come into contact with a new sort of power, namely, the power of the soul of man, which does continually intervene among the forces of nature, and produces effects aside from, and out of, the usual sequences of physical phenomena. All the triumphs of mechanics, of science, and of art have been won through the exercise of this power possessed by man, of bending the forces of nature to his will and using them in his service. We are continually reaching results which the forces of nature, left to themselves, never could have caused; and if this be so with men,

---

* See "The Mystery of Miracles," by the author of "The Supernatural in Nature," p. 15.

why should we deny to God the possibility of intervening in a similar way, and so producing effects that are not merely supernatural, but superhuman? The truth is, that if the personal existence of God be intelligently admitted, and if it be conceded that He is carrying on the operations of the universe by His power, there is no longer any foundation for the argument against the possibility of miracles, inasmuch as then they are seen to be only unusual manifestations of the same energy by which the common and ordinary processes of nature are maintained.

The verification of this is seen in the fact that, in recent days, the persistent antagonists of the supernatural have been driven either to the positive denial of the existence of God, or to that sad and dark Agnosticism which is sure of nothing, but that nothing can be known upon the subject. And in dealing with that, it might be enough to say with Bacon, that "God never wrought miracles to convince Atheism, because His ordinary works convince it."* The first postulate of Revelation is the being and personality of God—"In the beginning, God"—and we might almost be content to leave it where the Bible leaves it, without any formal attempt to confirm it by argument. But we can not forbear saying that the "I am" of human consciousness is in the soul,

---

* "Bacon's Essays, with Annotations by Richard Whately, D.D.," p. 188.

instinctively recognized as the echo of that greater "I AM" which Moses heard when he stood with unsandaled feet beside the burning bush.

In the same way, the experience of my own causative power disposes me to seek for a great first cause. It is to no purpose that Mr. Huxley affirms that "the origin of the elements of consciousness, no less than that of all its other states, is to be sought in bodily changes, the seat of which can only be placed in the brain;"* for though we admit the changes in the brain as connected with consciousness, it does not follow that they are the causes of it. A blush on the countenance is the common concomitant of the feeling of shame, but it is not the cause of that feeling; rather the spiritual condition, according to the consciousness of every one, is the cause of the physical change; and if that be so with an external appearance, the analogy leads us to conclude that the change in the brain itself is the result and not the cause of the spiritual emotion. But such a statement of such a philosopher is an illustration of the clean sweep which materialism would make, inasmuch as having ruled the spiritual God out of the universe, it rules also the spiritual nature out of man. But human nature will not let itself be thus outraged. It will insist on being something more than a mate-

---

* "Hume," by Professor Huxley, p. 74.

NATURE AND POSSIBILITY OF MIRACLES. 19

rial organization, and the consciousness of its own free volitional and causal power will impel it to seek for and worship a spiritual cause of the universe which it perceives.

Again, the exercise of my own intelligence and choice in the adaptation of means to ends, impels me irresistibly to conclude, from the discovery of similar adaptation in the works of nature, that there must have been a personal mind and will in the making of such an adjustment.

A few years ago great preparations were made by astronomers in Europe and America for the purpose of observing the transit of the planet Venus across the sun. The finest instruments were made, and parties went out to different places to take their several surveys. The whole thing was over in a few minutes; but all this mental activity of many human personalities was exerted to inspect it because of a certain relation between it and other phenomena, whereby the distance from the earth to the sun might be correctly calculated. Now, if all that adjustment of means to ends, arguing the design of a personal being, or rather of many personal beings, needed to be made for the purpose of observing the phenomenon, with what consistency can we deny that the phenomenon itself, and its relations to other phenomena, which made its careful inspection so important, were produced by a personal being? The truth is, when we see anywhere an adjustment of one thing to another for the purpose of securing a third thing, we are irresistibly impelled, or, at least, men generally (with the possible exception of a few agnostics) are impelled, in spite of themselves, to refer that adjustment to a personal and intelligent being, having both wisdom, and choice, and power. When, therefore, the philosopher says to me, "I have nothing to do with final causes, my business is simply with phenomena; I take cognizance only of observed appearances and ascertained connections;" I reply, that as an anatomist, a botanist, or a geologist, he may be right enough in so restricting himself, but, as a *man*, he can lay no such embargo upon his thoughts; for, whether he likes it or not, and as the result of his very manhood, final causes will force themselves upon his attention. As a man, he does always something more than observe and classify. In spite of himself, as even the writings of our materialistic philosophers abundantly illustrate, he seeks to go behind and beneath phenomena for some explanation of the facts. Besides, as one has said very beautifully here, "There are relations between himself and the universe which no analysis of sensuous observations can exhaust. The starry sky has some nameless grandeur which no results of mathematical calculation can express. The tender clouds, whose colors he analyzes in his prism, speak a language to his heart which no prismatic chart can interpret. And among such incalculable relations between himself and the universe is the wistful longing after inner meaning and ultimate aim which the enigma of creation always excites in the contemplative soul. Most natural is the artless hymn which represents the young child as appealing to the little star on high, and exclaiming, 'How I wonder what you are!' So all our life long we stand at gaze, the vision expanding from a star to a universe, while still all our cry is of wonder what is. And this inquiry after what is, includes manifestly a longing after the significance and purpose of appearances; that is, it involves the hunger of the soul for a final cause of creation."* Thus the instinctive yearning of the soul, strengthened and made intelligent by the experience of its own operations in causation and design, leads us inevitably to a great intelligent cause, "of whom, and to whom, and through whom are all things."

But to some it may seem as if the modern hypothesis of development or evolution, militated conclusively against the personal existence and agency of God as the sustainer of all things; and so left no place for the supernatural, because it has no place for God. The fact, however, that this hypothesis has been adopted, and is advocated by men, some of

---

* J. A. Picton, "New Theories and the Old Faith," pp. 7, 8.

whom are devout believers in the God and Father of our Lord Jesus Christ, shows that it is not essentially atheistic; though, undoubtedly, it is held by many who have no place for God in their philosophy.* To me it seems that even if it were conclusively proved to be true, which, however, is still very far from being the case, the argument for the existence of God from design, would not lose one particle of its strength. For where it is held in conjunction with atheism, its votaries have been guilty of the fallacy which we have already exposed in connection with the word law. They have taken a whole class of results, and made the formulized expression of that, the cause of the production of these results. They have named their law the survival of the fittest, and have supposed that thereby they have accounted for the peculiar fitness of each permanent species to survive, which is, of course, absurd. I have never seen this thought so powerfully put as by the late Canon Mozley, who thus reasons: "Natural selection is not an agent at all, but a result. It is the effect which proceeds from a favorable modification or development of structure in one animal, in the struggle for existence with another animal not thus additionally endowed, viz, his survivorship and continuance on the field while the other per-

---

* See Appendix A.

ishes."* But whence has come this favorable modification or development? As Mozley goes on to say, "The favored party in this struggle, the party that lives would have lived all the same if there had been no struggle for existence and no natural selection; and he does not owe his existence and continuance to natural selection, he only owes his sole existence to it as distinguished from the fate of a rival who perishes."† So far, therefore, as the question of causation is concerned, natural selection leaves it where it found it. It does not itself account for the appearance of the fittest; but only for the disappearance of the unfit in what is called "the struggle for existence," and it leaves as much room for, nay, it as inexorably demands the presence of a presiding and overruling mind, as does the old decried theory of special creation. Hence, in reply to those who, when we speak of the supernatural, meet us with the theory of development—we take our stand again on the instinctive yearning of the human soul for a cause for every effect, and we say, "Suppose we admit your hypothesis, then we are still impelled to ask, whence came the primordial germ out of which all that we see, as well as all that we are, is said to have sprung? How could there be evolution without pre-

---

* Canon Mozley's Essays, Historical and Theological, Vol. II., p. 396.
† Ibid, p. 396. See Appendix B.

vious involution? Who, then, put into that protoplasm the "promise and the potency" of all that has ultimately come out of it? Let us concede the facts from the analogy of which your theory of natural selection has been suggested: the inquiry still arises, must there not be, according to the analogy of these facts—notably that of the pigeon breeder, for instance—some mind or will presiding to regulate the selection? Let us grant that there is some foundation for the law which has been called the "survival of the fittest," then the irrepressible question still leaps to the lips, whence came this "fittest-ness" for surviving? Has it been the result of chance? or, must there not have been a presiding intelligence who in accordance with that law is carrying forward his purposes and working out his will?

Moreover, if there be such a great gulf fixed between that which is destitute of life, and that which possesses life, that, on the confession of the most illustrious naturalists, no process yet known to man, or observed in nature, has been able to bridge it, whence came life? If life must have its origin in life, must there not be, high over all natural developments, one who is emphatically the living one, having life in himself and quickening whom he will? and is there not in the first appearance of life in what you call development, that which is, on your own showing, a miracle—namely, a work out of the usual sequence of secondary causes and effects, and produced by an agency from without, or what we call the agency of God?

So, in vindicating the existence and personality of a living God from those who hold the doctrine of development in an atheistic form, we have found both an answer to them, and taking them on their own ground a miracle in the far past, which proves at least the possibility of such occurrences; while we trust that we have made it apparent that the affirmation of the impossibility of a miracle carries with it the elimination of God out of the universe, and of the spirit out of man.

THE SUPERNATURAL IN CHRIST.

LECTURE II.

THE SUPERNATURAL IN CHRIST.

John xiv. 11 : Believe me that I am in the Father and the Father in me ; or else believe me for the very works' sake.

IN dealing with the question of the credibility of miracles, two methods, each of which is independent of the other, and satisfactory in itself, may be adopted. We may either begin with the character and personality of the miracle-worker, and draw from these such conclusions as shall warrant us in accepting as genuine the mighty works which He performed, inasmuch as they are in perfect keeping with the great object which He had in view, and such as it was not only possible, but natural that *He* should do ; or we may start from the contemplation of the miracles themselves, and taking into consideration the testimony by which they are supported, the character of the witnesses by whom that testimony is borne, and the absurdity of the position into which we shall be driven if such testimony should be treated as false, we may rise through the works to the recognition of the divine personality of Him who wrought them. We may look first at the character of Jesus

Christ himself, and from an investigation of that, altogether irrespective, for the time being, of His miracles, we may find reason to believe that He is indeed "God manifest in the flesh." That gives us the Incarnation, which is not only in itself a miracle, but also the explanation and vindication of all the miracles which Christ performed; for from the elevation which that supplies, these wonderful works are seen to be natural to Him, as but the forth-puttings, on proper occasions, and for sufficient reasons, of the omnipotence which is one of the attributes of Deity. Or taking up the works themselves as facts attested by evidence sufficient to establish the occurrence even of such marvellous things, we may see in them the Divine endorsement of the doctrines He taught, and of the claims He made, and so through them reach to the faith, expressed by Thomas, when, as the reality of the miracle of the resurrection of Christ was apprehended by him, he said, "My Lord and my God."

The miracles are thus, from one point of view, the natural accompaniments of the Incarnation; and from another, the evidences of the fact that Jesus is Incarnate God. Nor let any one suppose that these two methods of looking at them are incompatible with each other. They are independent of each other, but not inconsistent with each other; and it seems to me that they are both sanctioned by the words of Jesus Christ himself. Thus in His last conversation with His followers, when Philip asked Him to show them the Father, He replied: "He that hath seen me hath seen the Father, and how sayest thou, then, show us the Father? Believest thou not that I am in the Father, and the Father in me? The words that I speak unto you, I speak not of myself; but the Father that dwelleth in me, he doeth the works. Believe me that I am in the Father and the Father in me, or else (or if not) believe me for the very works' sake."* To the same effect is His vindication of Himself from the charge of blasphemy brought against Him by the Jews, when He said : "I and my Father are one;" thus, "If I do not the works of my Father, believe me not; but if I do, though ye believe not me, believe the works, that ye may know and believe that the Father is in me, and I in him." † Thus alike to His friends and to His enemies, Jesus put forth Himself as one with the Father. If they had such appreciation of His character as to see His Godhead through that, then they had at once the best of reasons for believing Him ; but if they could not reach such a height by the mere contemplation of Himself, then the supernatural works which He performed might serve as a stairway up which they might ascend to the reception of Him as Incarnate God.

* John xiv. 9-11.   † Ibid. x. 38

These two methods of arriving at virtually the same result are separate and independent processes; they are not contradictory. The one does not interfere with the other, or build on anything which needs first to be established by the other. We may therefore take either according to the object which we have in view, or we may employ both, if, for any reason, it may seem expedient that we should do so. Now, there is one good reason why we may seek, in these discourses, to formulate, amplify, and illustrate both; for there are two orders of minds among men which correspond to these two methods. On the one hand, we have the reflective type, which is most easily moved by that which lays hold on the moral nature, and is impressed more deeply by that which is revealed through character than by any merely physical manifestation of power. On individuals of that order, the perception of the moral miracle in the life of Jesus is more effective than any argument drawn even from His resurrection from the dead. On the other hand, we have the perceptive type, which is influenced by things occurring before the eyes, or by effects that are startling to the senses, and inexplicable by ordinary physical laws, more than by moral or spiritual manifestations; and for those of this class the supernatural works wrought by Christ become, when satisfactorily established, the means of leading them to faith in Him as "the true God and Eternal Life."

Every age of the Church has seen minds of both these orders. In one age, indeed, the one has seemed to have pre-eminence, and in another, the other; but always there have been some of each, and sometimes the same individual has passed through both phases. At first, in the outset of his inquiries into the Gospel narratives, he has sympathized with Nicodemus, and has gone to Jesus in the faith that no man could do such miracles as He did except God were with him; but as the years have rolled on, and the glory of Christ's character has grown upon him, through his own growth in every grace, he has felt himself thinking less and less of the miracles as works of power. They are no stumbling-blocks to him, indeed; but they enter less consciously into his thoughts than they did before. He rests in his conviction that Christ is the "Word" made "flesh," whose glory is "full of grace and truth;" and though he got to that conviction at the first through the miracles, he retains it now, without much reference to them, but because of his increasing appreciation of the Christ himself. The works have become almost secondary things, in his realization of the Deity of the worker.

I believe many of us are conscious of having passed through an experience like that. But something of the same sort has occurred in the history of the Church of Christ as a whole. In the beginning, the impression made by the miracles was very strong.

The men who actually saw them never could forget the effect which was produced upon them by the sight. But as the witnesses gradually passed away and left only their testimony behind them, very naturally the vividness of the result was diminished; and we do not find that any reader of the account of the first miraculous draft of fishes was ever stimulated thereby to cry with Peter, when he saw it, "Depart from me, for I am a sinful man, O Lord." This, however, is largely compensated by the fact, that in proportion as the freshness of the impression first produced by the sight of Christ's miracles has worn off, the character and influence of Christ himself have become increasingly operative among men, and are to-day the most potent forces at work on humanity at large. They who lived beside Him were too close upon Him to see all that His character implied; for them, therefore, the miracles were, in the startlingness of their effects, exceedingly helpful in giving them a right appreciation of His mission. But as the centuries have rolled on, and brought out, strangely enough, only the more distinctly as they have advanced, the majesty of Christ himself, we find now that the personality of Christ is the great solvent of His miracles. It enables us to understand, explain, and defend them; and, after our acceptance of Him, we have little or no hesitation about receiving them.

I think I can see evidences that in the apostolic

THE SUPERNATURAL IN CHRIST. 35

age itself a transition of the kind which I have indicated had passed, at least, over one of the Evangelists. The first gospels abound in miracles to a far greater extent than the last. That of Mark, the earliest, as it is generally believed, of the four, gives special prominence to them; that of Matthew presents us with some of the most important discourses, but still the miracles occupy what may be regarded as the most conspicuous place; that of Luke, which came still later, partakes of the same character, though by the introduction of those parables, which are peculiar to him, this evangelist shows us that he had attained a deeper insight than his predecessors into the heart of Christ. But that of John puts the Incarnation first, for by the time he came to write it, the aged apostle had grown to a larger apprehension of the character of his Lord, and it is his aim throughout it to let that character appear and speak for itself. So we account for the fact, that in the fourth gospel, we have the record of comparatively few miracles,* and even these few are described, not so much for their own sake, or for the sake of the evidence which they gave to Christ, as because they were the starting-points of those discourses wherein Jesus gave the brightest testimony to Himself. The increased distance between him and the

---

* Only eight, exclusive of His resurrection.

date of the Lord's life, helped John to see better the transcending glory of that life; and he was more intent on showing that to his readers than on giving a series of miracles. I do not know whether I have discovered the right explanation; but, whether I have or not, the fact is apparent, that the latest of the four gospels contains the record of the fewest miracles, and that of itself ought to be conclusive against the theory which would make the stories of the miracles myths, which grew around the popular conception of Christ among the members of the Church. The truth seems rather to have been, that the miracles at first assumed the prominence, and then gradually receded into a secondary place as men gained an impression of the grander miracle which was presented in the character of Christ.

It will not seem strange to you, therefore, that of the two methods which I have described, I should begin with the first. We take that miracle which is existing and operating yet before our eyes and in the midst of us—the supernatural in Christ—and we find in the establishment of that the proof that the mighty works here recorded are credible.

I base my argument, here, on two facts which are patent to every observer. On the one hand, we have in these gospels, the miracles for the time being altogether apart, the record of a life, of which the external surroundings may be thus described. In the most degenerate age of Jewish history, when immorality was undermining the foundations of the Roman ascendancy throughout the world, a young man born in Bethlehem, and educated after the ordinary fashion of His nation, in a district which was proverbial for its coarseness, and a village which was a by-word for its wickedness, wrought as a common carpenter till He was thirty years of age. Then for three years and a half He wandered up and down His native land claiming to be received and listened to as a teacher, and having as His immediate attendants a few fishermen, tax-gathers, and men of no liberal education. For a time He had a large following among the common people; but the incisive sharpness of His moral discourses so cut the hearts of the rulers, that at last they laid hold of Him, and, with the connivance—say rather, through the instrumentality—of the Roman governor of the province, they secured His crucifixion. These are facts which not even the wildest scepticism has ever attempted to deny or to call in question.

On the other hand, it is equally incontrovertible, that the history of that young man as written by His followers has been the most powerful force in human history ever since its promulgation among men; and that His name is to-day worshipped among millions, while even by those who stop short of worship it is venerated as that of the greatest of the sons of men. Before four centuries had passed away, and that too in the face of repeated persecutions of His disciples by the Imperial power, the spiritual might of that history made itself felt throughout the Roman Empire, and took possession of the Imperial throne itself; and to-day, before our own eyes, even at the distance of eighteen centuries from the events, it is more active than ever, and seems gathering to itself new energy for yet grander triumphs than any which it has yet achieved. All through these successive years that history has sat among men like its great subject by the well of Sychar, telling them all things that ever they did, discerning the very thoughts of their hearts, and leading them to a higher life than without it, they had ever dreamed of entering upon. Under its influence the drunkard has become sober, the thief has become honest, the adulterer has become chaste, the selfish has become disinterested. It has gone into the homes of men and turned, there, the water of mere earthly fellowship into the wine of spiritual communion, making each household where its supremacy is recognized, like that of Bethany, a dwelling-place in which the studies of the Maries are hallowed because they are carried on at Jesus' feet; and the ministrations of the Marthas are dignified because they are rendered unto Him. It has taken the little children into its arms and blessed them; recognizing their existence with its smile and marking their importance by its attention. It has been to society

—excuse the illustration, for I can get nothing but a miracle that really resembles it—like the tree which Moses cast into the bitter fountain, and has sweetened and purified all the relationships of men to men. It has gone into political life, and by that great word," Render unto Cæsar the things that are Cæsar's, and unto God the things that are God's," it has contended successfully for liberty of conscience while upholding human government, and thereby it has laid also the foundations, broad and indestructible, of civil freedom. It has stood between class and class as the good Samaritan of humanity, and has succored and revived those who had been maltreated, and all but murdered by the grasping avarice and cruel mammonism of their fellows. It has, in fine, been the consoler of the race, amid all the cares and sorrows to which men are heirs. It has wiped the tears from the eyes of the mourner as he stood by the grave that was soon to cover in the remains of one he tenderly and truly loved; it has soothed the pain of the afflicted one as he lay on his bed of anguish; it has given a song to the oppressed in the dark night of his imprisonment or slavery; and, as the death damp has stood upon the brow, and the glaze of dissolution has dimmed the eye, it has given not only peace, but positive triumph to untold multitudes of men.

These also are facts which no man will deny. We have seen them ourselves. Some of us have had personal experiences which are their best attestations. Any man who cares to go to the right places to seek for them, may witness them to-night in multitudinous instances in the cities of our land. Nor have they been confined to any one age, or class, or country. The power of this story has been proved in every century. It has been as manifest among the erudite and the elevated, as among the illiterate and the lowly. It has lost nothing by its reproduction even in the rudest languages, but its efficacy has been demonstrated among the Hindoos and the Hottentots, the Chinese and the South Sea Islanders, as really as among the Anglo-Saxons of Europe and America. Its influence is over men as men, and wherever among men that influence has begun to work, it has had a distinctive and peculiar effect, like to nothing else that has ever been operative among them. It has quickened them, intellectually, morally, and spiritually, so that it may well be said to have put a new life into them. But lest you should think that with my inevitable prepossessions, I am exaggerating in speaking thus, I will fortify myself here with a quotation from the writings of one who is at least above all such suspicion in that regard. I mean Mr. Lecky, who, in his " History of Morality from Augustus to Charlemagne," has written thus : " It was reserved for Christianity to present to the world an ideal character, which, through all the changes of eighteen centuries has filled the hearts

THE SUPERNATURAL IN CHRIST. 41

of men with an impassioned love, and has shown itself capable of acting on all ages, nations, temperaments, and conditions; has not only been the highest pattern of virtue, but the highest incentive to its practice, and has exerted so deep an influence that it may be truly said that the simple record of three short years of active life has done more to regenerate and to soften mankind than all the disquisitions of philosophers, and than all the exhortations of moralists. This has indeed been the well-spring of whatever has been best and purest in the Christian life. Amid all the sins and failings, amid all the priestcraft, the persecution, and fanaticism which have defaced the Church, it has preserved in the character and example of its Founder an enduring principle of regeneration."*

Now, taking on the one hand the external surroundings of the life of Jesus, as I have set them before you, and on the other the influence of that life on humanity, I ask, Have we in the former, viewed simply by themselves, and as destitute of any supernatural element, anything like an adequate explanation of the latter? If Jesus was only a Jewish artisan, who died at thirty-three, how could His life-record have thus revolutionized all history? We are commonly supposed in these days and in this country

---

* Vol. II., p. 8, quoted in Row's Bampton Lecture, p. 96.

to live more in a brief time than the ancients did in one that, reckoned by days and years, was longer. But which of those who have done anything to shape the course of our history would have had even the opportunity of doing so if he had died at the age of thirty-three? Not Washington, not Webster, not Lincoln. No matter, therefore, what a man's other advantages may be; nay, even in connection with the highest human advantages, a sufficiently long term of life must be recognized as essential to the exercise by him of such an influence as shall make its mark deep and permanent on the character and history of a nation, much more of the world. How, then, shall we explain the fact that the mightiest regenerative force which has been exerted on our race came out of a life which was cut off almost in youth, and whose public work was performed in the space of three years and a half? From the distinctive character of the effects produced by it, I am warranted in concluding that there was something peculiar and unique in the personality of Him by whom they were produced. They are such effects, not only in degree, but in kind, as no other's man's life before or since, save as connected with His, has generated. They have amounted, on Mr. Lecky's own showing, to a regeneration of mankind, and therefore I am compelled to infer that He who is the regenerator of men is something more than a man. There must have been more in Him than in the race, else He could not have thus told upon the race. Water cannot rise above its source; immorality cannot produce morality; that which is hastening to decay cannot renew itself, and its renewal must be the result of the introduction into it of something higher, nobler, and more powerful than itself.

The force of these considerations has been felt even by those who have refused to recognize anything like a divine element in Jesus; and some of them have sought to account, on merely natural principles, for the remarkable effects which we have described. Thus Gibbon, in his celebrated fifteenth chapter, has enumerated five secondary causes (intending, however, that his readers should recognize them as primary) for the rapid diffusion and wide acceptance of Christianity. These, as all of you must know, were the inflexible zeal of the Christians, the doctrine of a future life, the miraculous powers ascribed to the primitive Church, the pure and austere morals of the Christians, and the union and discipline of the Christian republic. But all these, with the exception of the third—the miraculous powers ascribed to the primitive Church—are themselves effects which need to be accounted for, and so the admission of their operation does not at all lessen the difficulty; while in regard to the third, it may be said that, if the miraculous powers ascribed to the primitive Church were real, they lead back to the miraculous in Christ; but if they were false, we have the palpable absurdity, not to say impossibility, of ascribing pure and austere morals to the adherents of a system founded on deception. Very evidently, therefore, these secondary causes are not adequate to solve the problem.

Mr. Mill, again, is satisfied with the affirmation that the genius and moral qualities of Jesus are sufficient to account for all the effects which we have described. Here are his words, and very remarkable words they are as coming from him: "About the life and sayings of Jesus there is a stamp of personal originality combined with profundity of insight, which, if we abandon the idle expectation of finding scientific precision, where something very different was aimed at, must place the prophet of Nazareth, even in the estimation of those who have no belief in His inspiration, in the very first rank of the men of sublime genius of whom our species can boast. When this pre-eminent genius is combined with the qualities of probably the greatest moral reformer and martyr to that mission who ever existed upon earth, religion cannot be said to have made a bad choice in pitching on this man as the ideal representative and guide of humanity; nor even now would it be easy, even for an unbeliever, to find a better translation of the rule of virtue from the abstract into the concrete, than to endeavor so to live that Christ would approve our life."* But, I submit, that it is not possible to go so far as this, without, for the sake of logical consistency, going much farther. For genius alone will not account for the effect which even Mr. Mill recognizes was produced on men by the life of Christ; no, not even when it is allied with the qualities of a moral reformer and a martyr. Even if we admit that such genius as Jesus possessed is not itself the very thing to be accounted for, considering the surroundings of his youth and manhood, it remains a fact that the world has never been regenerated by genius, or moved to offer such homage to those who were dowered with it, as men pay to Jesus. Homer did not become a deity to the Greeks, nor Virgil to the Romans. No name of genius is more honored to-day in Germany than that of Goethe; but what a difference is there between the feelings of his admirers toward him and those cherished—I will not say merely by Christians, but by the world at large—toward Jesus? At the mention of the name of Robert Burns every Scotchman's "blood" (to use his own words regarding Wallace) "boils up in a springtide flood;" but who thinks of him as a regenerator of society? or who would organize a mission to carry his life-story to heathen nations? Probably the most cosmopolitan specimen of genius the world has ever

---

* "Three Essays in Religion," by J. S. Mill, pp. 254, 255.

seen was that of William Shakespeare; but who does not feel as wide a divergence between his writings, admirable as they are, and these four gospels, as there is between the electric light and a star; between the finest specimens of the architect's handiwork and the magnificent cathedral rocks that rise sheer and high on the side of the Yosemite? for the one is human in its origin, and the other is the handiwork of God.

Nay, even when to the element of genius we add those of the moral reformer and the martyr, we are not perceptibly nearer giving any adequate explanation of the effects produced on humanity by the life of Christ than we were before. For we find genius, reforming energy, and martyrdom all combined in the story of Socrates, which always, as I read it, seems to me to constitute the high-water mark of mere unaided manhood. But what is Socrates to men to-day? what churches have been founded for his worship? what missionary associations have been instituted for the translation and diffusion of the Phædo, the Crito, and the Apology? and who among the children of men is moved to abstain from doing wrong, or to persevere in doing right, for the sake of the son of Sophroniscus? while, on the other hand, with a vast multitude of mankind, there is no motive so powerful as the "for my sake," from the lips of the Son of Mary. There is here, therefore, in the life of Christ, some quality that is not found in manhood, as such. What is that quality, if it is not supernatural? What is it, if it is not Divine? It is, at least, all history being the witness, superhuman; and yet it has become so mighty on our race, because the superhuman operated through One who, whatever else He was, was also really a man. Here is a moral miracle which renders credible the physical signs and wonders with which its manifestation to men was accompanied.

But the force of this argument increases when, looking away from the mere surroundings of Christ's life, we examine the character which the Evangelists have here portrayed. It is one of absolute moral perfection. He said, "Which of you convicteth me of sin?"* And as we read the history we are not shocked to hear such words from Him, for they but give voice to the impression which we ourselves derive from the whole narrative. His meekness and gentleness were only equalled by His honesty and benevolence. There was about Him a conscientious thoroughness which was carried out at every sacrifice; and so far from having that love of ostentation which might be expected in One so marvellously endowed, there was a disposition to shun the applause of popularity and the blaze of earthly glory. His Sermon on the Mount evinces that, above and beyond all other things in religion, He delighted in

---

* John viii. 46.

"truth in the inward parts," and held in utter abhorrence that cold and hollow ritualism which is content with the form of godliness while denying its power. Never was there such an equipoise of moral attributes as we find in Him. To an all-embracing benevolence, He joined a sternness of principle which exposed wrong wherever He found it, and insisted on faithfulness in that which was least. But most of all, pervading His other qualities and shedding its own bright halo round them all, was His self-sacrificing and devoted love, manifest in the price He paid and the zeal He showed for the redemption and regeneration of men. Unlike that Socrates, "whom well inspired, the oracle pronounced wisest of men," but who went to the house of the strange woman and gave her advice on the best means of prosecuting her vile business, and of winning and keeping her friends, Jesus restored to the woman of the city "the piece which she had lost," and sent her away to live a life of purity and holiness. No dishonor darkens His name; no scandal fastened itself on His renown. Before the portrait which these Evangelists have painted, men of every age have stood in rooted admiration; and as we have seen in the case of men like Lecky and Mill, even by those who, however inconsistently, deny His deity, He is held in estimation as the noblest of men. For centuries His life has been the object of the keenest investigation;

"through all this tract of years" men have looked at Him

> "In that fierce light which beats upon a throne
> And blackens every blot;"

but still they have seen in Him, and that, too, in a far higher sense than the poet has employed the words, only " the white flower of a blameless life."

Now, how shall we account for the existence of such a character as a literary portrait, but from its historical reality? Even Mr. Mill himself has made this acknowledgment in these words: "It is of no use to say that Christ, as exhibited in the gospels, is not historical;" and again, "Who among His disciples or among their proselytes was capable of inventing the sayings ascribed to Jesus, or of imagining the life and character revealed in the gospels? Certainly not the fishermen of Galilee; certainly not St. Paul, whose character and idiosyncrasies were of a totally different sort; still less the early Christian writers, in whom nothing is more evident than that the good which was in them was all derived, as they always professed that it was derived, from a higher source."*

But if it were real and historical, could it have been merely human? For now, in connection with this admission of His moral pre-eminence, we must take

---

* "Three Essays in Religion," *ub sup.*, pp. 253, 254.

notice of certain very remarkable things associated with it. For His was a piety, with no consciousness of sin, and with no profession of repentance. Never does Jesus confess Himself a sinner; nowhere does He utter a word of penitence; therefore His perfection is of a different nature from that which it is possible for any sinner to attain; and knowing, as we do, how much the depravity of the race implies, we must acknowledge that we have here a supernatural breaking in upon the course of human nature, and must recognize a miracle in Christ himself.

Still further, this moral perfection was associated with certain claims to something higher than humanity. He declared Himself to be the Messiah. He claimed "power on earth to forgive sins."* He affirmed that He and the Father were one, and took no means to keep the Jews from inferring therefrom that He "made himself God."† He alleged that He would be the final judge of the living and the dead;‡ and in the very moment of making the profession that He was "meek and lowly in heart," He gave the invitation, "Come unto me, all ye that labor and are heavy laden, and I will give you rest," which has in it the assumption of the prerogative of Deity.§ He was Himself the topic of all His discourses; and the "I say unto you," of the Sermon on the Mount is,

---

* Mark ii. 10. † John x. 30–38. ‡ John v. 21–29; Matt. xxv. 31
§ Matt. xi. 28–30.

in this aspect, not more remarkable than the "I am the water of life," "I am the bread of life," "I am the light of the world," "I am the door," "I am the good shepherd," "I am the resurrection and the life," "I am the way, the truth, and the life," "I am the true vine," which give its distinctive characteristic to the fourth gospel. Now, how shall we reconcile moral perfection, or even moral excellence, short of perfection, and such as we expect from a moral reformer with these claims? Only by admitting that they were true. If they are true, then He is incarnate God. If they are not true, then He is not merely a man, but a man dishonored and debased by the utterance of falsehoods in matters of highest human concernment, and so far from being worthy of the homage of mankind, that He deserves their reprobation. If they are not true, then the force which He continues to exert in history is incomprehensible. If they are not true, then the mightiest incentives to holiness have come from One who was Himself a deceiver; and the noblest influence for the purification of humanity has emanated from One who, when He said "I am the truth," was expressing either a delusion or a lie. Verily that is a kind of development which even science should brand as an impossibility; but the branding of it thus is an admission of the Deity of Christ, and so an establishment of the credibility of the miracles that He wrought.

Still again, and apart from the influence of Christ's claims, when taken in connection with His moral perfection, let us set that perfection in the environment of His age, and ask how it is to be accounted for. As I have casually remarked already, it was an age of corruption everywhere. Society throughout the entire Roman Empire was honeycombed with vileness. The very worship of the gods was made to minister to the lowest passions of man's nature. Woman was degraded, infanticide was frequent, and "things which it were a shame even to name," but which Paul has simply hinted at in that awful passage in the Epistle to the Romans,* were common in all the great cities at the time; while the very amusements of the people were steeped in cruelty, and multitudes were "butchered to make a holiday." Nor was Judæa an exception, save in a very minor degree, to the rest of the Empire. The revelation by Moses and the prophets, indeed, had made some change; but the revival under the Maccabees had been succeeded by an age of luxury and vice, just as the earnestness of the time of the English Commonwealth was followed by lasciviousness unparallelled in British history; for Josephus affirms that "the land was full of robberies," and that at "no time of their history had the nation been more wretched." What

---

* Rom. i. 19–25.

THE SUPERNATURAL IN CHRIST. 53

was there in that age, then, to produce or develop out of itself such a character as Christ's? Even if we accept the theory of development in history, as in other things, we must have gradual upward approaches toward the completed type of excellence which is finally reached. But where are these approaches here? In the very darkest age the light appeared; in the most depraved period of human history, morally speaking at least, this type of moral perfection was manifested.

How shall we account for that? Do not tell me that Jesus Christ was the outgrowth of His times. Take Rome before the advent with Cicero as a representative of its philosophy and statesmanship, Horace as the popular idol among its poets, and Clodius as a specimen of its morals; take Greece, with its different sects of philosophy, Stoics, Epicureans, Platonists, and the like; take Judaism, whether as seen at Alexandria among the disciples of Philo, or in Judæa among the formal Pharisees, the sceptical Sadducees, or the ascetic Essenes. Put all these into the crucible of such an age as that undeniably was, and by what amalgam known to men could these elements have produced Jesus Christ? The legitimate child of that age was the dilletante litterateur, the amateur musician, the fashionable charioteer, the cruel monster—Nero. But so far from being a development of His generation, Jesus was crucified by His generation for being what He was; and the inscription over His cross, written as it was in letters of Hebrew, and Greek, and Latin, may fitly symbolize the agreement of all the three nationalities in putting Him to death. He was no development of His age; but instead, everything true and noble and loving and godlike in succeeding generations has been developed out of Him; and so in Him a supernatural, superhuman element must have resided, or, in other words, there must have been a miracle in His very personality. And if we accept that, the simplest form of such a miracle, mysterious as it is, is the Incarnation of Deity in the human nature which He wore.

But to bring this argument to a close, let me pivot the whole question on a single instance. The skillful naturalist can sometimes from but one fragment of a fossil animal reconstruct for us its entire organism, and tell us of its abode, its habits, and its classification. So it seems to me, that from one remarkable utterance of Jesus, we are able to establish to all candid minds the fact that He is God incarnate. Take then that prayer which we find in the seventeenth chapter of John's Gospel, and try to account on rational principles for its simple existence. It contains such sentences as these: " Glorify thy Son, that thy Son also may glorify thee: as thou hast given him power over all flesh, that he should give eternal life to as many as thou hast given him. And this is life eternal, that they might know thee, the only true God, and Jesus Christ whom thou hast sent." "And now, O Father, glorify thou me with thine own self, with the glory which I had with thee before the world was." "Father, I will that they also whom thou hast given me be with me where I am; that they may behold my glory which thou hast given me." Now, whence has come the prayer in which these sentences occur? It is conceivable, but barely conceivable, that an insane man might have uttered the phrases which I have quoted, but then he who offered the rest of the prayer was evidently very far indeed from insanity, and therefore we can not accept the theory which would account for it on that hypothesis. Again, a bad man could not have presented that prayer, for it would have been impossible for him to have invented or conceived the situation out of which it rose, or to have produced such pure and holy sentiments as are expressed in the supplication when taken as a whole. But if a bad man could not have invented it, a good man would not. For a good man on his knees is full of humility, and the better he is as a man, the farther he is from saying that he has power over all flesh, that he gives eternal life to any one, or that eternal life in any sense consists in the knowledge of himself. But if a bad man could not, and a good man would not have invented this prayer, how comes it to be here? It is, I maintain, unthinkable by a merely human soul. Before it was uttered by Jesus no man could ever have conceived of the things which it expresses. There is that about it which demonstrates that he who uttered it was more than man. It carries on it the indication that it came out of a unique personality; it bears the impress of the Incarnation on its face, and proves that he who offered it was both really God and truly man. I maintain that it is impossible to account for its existence on any other principle, and thus the chapter which is composed by it, may well be called the Holy of Holies of the Gospel, for it shows, indeed, the radiance of the shechinah glory, which in symbol was over the ancient ark, but in reality abode in, and shone through, the person of Jesus Christ.

Now, these different lines of argument which I have prosecuted may be thus summed up. Taking the life of Christ in its external surroundings, and in connection with its influence on humanity at large; taking the moral perfection of Christ in connection with the claims which He put forth, and with the utter immorality of the age in which He appeared; taking the fabric of the prayer which we have just been considering in connection with the question, how it came into existence, we have a series of problems presented, for which no adequate natural explanation can be found; but which are at once fully and perfectly accounted for on the hypothesis, put forth in the proem of John's gospel, that Jesus of Nazareth is "the word made flesh;" or, in other words, INCARNATE GOD. That key fits every ward in the lock; no other can be got to enter it all, and so on the principles of the Inductive Philosophy itself, we have a right to hold that marvellous, mysterious, miraculous as it is, that is the true solution.

But now, when we have accepted that, behold how the miracles of these narratives fall into their proper places, and are seen to be the natural accompaniments of the greater moral miracle in Christ himself. If He is God, we cannot wonder that He trod the waves in triumph; commanded the winds into peace; multiplied the loaves and fishes; healed the sick; and raised the dead. For these "signs" to us are only "works" to God. That which is supernatural to us is just as easy to Him as is the upholding of the regular course of nature. We have in Him, taken as the God-man, a cause adequate to the production of such effects; and we have in the fact of His appearing among men as their Redeemer an occasion worthy of their manifestation. The one great miracle is the Incarnation, and that once accepted, everything else in the narratives of the Gospel becomes natural, and only what in the circumstances might have been expected.

I conclude in the words of Bushnell, which sum up

3*

the substance of what I have been trying to say: "If the miracles, if revelation itself cannot stand upon the superhuman character of Jesus, then let it fall. If that character does not contain all truth in itself, then let there be no truth. If there is anything worthy of belief not found in this, we may well consent to live and die without it. Before this sovereign light, streaming out from God, the deep questions and dark surmisings and doubts unresolved, which make a night so gloomy and terrible about us, hurry away to their native abyss. God, who commanded the light to shine out of darkness, hath shined in our hearts to give the light of the knowledge to the glory of God in the face of Jesus Christ. This it is that has conquered the assaults of doubt and false learning in all past ages, and will in all ages to come. No argument against the sun will drive it from the sky. No mole-eyed scepticism, dazzled by its brightness, can turn away the shining it refuses to look upon. And they who long after God will be ever turning their eyes thitherward, and either with reason or without reason, or, if need be, against manifold impediments of reason will see and believe."*

---

* "Nature and the Supernatural," pp. 365, 366.

THE CREDIBILITY OF MIRACLES.

LECTURE III.

THE CREDIBILITY OF MIRACLES.

Acts xxvi. 8 : Why should it be thought a thing incredible with you, that God should raise the dead?

LEAVING the argument of our last lecture to stand distinct and independent, I propose now, for the satisfaction of the second class of minds which I then described, to take up the question from the other side; and, beginning with the miracles and the testimony by which they are supported, to proceed to the consideration of the evidence which they give to the claims advanced, and the doctrine, taught by Him who wrought them.

But here our right of way is disputed at the very outset by those who declare that no amount of proof can establish the occurrence of a miracle; and at their head is David Hume, with the argument of that famous Essay which has not been, in any material respect, improved upon by any of those who have come after him; but, on the contrary, has only been reproduced under different terminology, even by the most recent antagonists of the Gospel. It is not, therefore, a work of supererogation, far less a slaying of the slain, to expose what I believe to be its utter sophistry, and so establish our right to the examination of the testimony which he deliberately refuses to admit into the case.

I begin with reproducing, mainly in Hume's own words, the argument itself: "Experience is our only guide in reasoning concerning matters of fact."* Experience is in some things variable, in some things uniform. A variable experience gives rise only to a probability; a uniform experience amounts to a proof. Probability always supposes an opposition of experiments and observations, where the one side is found to overbalance the other, and to produce a degree of evidence proportioned to the superiority.† In such cases we must balance the opposite experiments, and deduct the lesser number from the greater, in order to know the exact force of the superior evidence.‡ Our assurance in regard to any species of reasoning which is derived from the reports of eye-witnesses, "is derived from no other principle than our observation of the veracity of human testimony, and of the usual conformity of facts to the reports of witnesses."§ But "suppose that the fact which the testimony endeavors to establish, partakes of the extraordinary and the marvellous; in that case, the evidence resulting from the testimony, admits of a diminution, greater

---
* Hume's Essays, Green and Grose's edition, 1875. Vol. II. p. 89.
† Ibid., pp. 90, 91.   ‡ Ibid., p. 90.   § Ibid., p. 90.

or less, in proportion as the fact is more or less unusual. The reason why we place any credit in witnesses and historians, is not derived from any connection which we perceive *a priori*, between testimony and reality, but because we are accustomed to find a conformity between them. But when the fact attested is such an one as has seldom fallen under our observation, here is a contest of two opposite experiences, of which the one destroys the other, as far as its force goes, and the superior can only operate in the mind by the force which remains."* Further, if the fact affirmed by the witnesses, "instead of being only marvellous is really miraculous," and if besides "the testimony, considered apart and in itself amounts to an entire proof; in that case, there is proof against proof, of which the strongest must prevail, but still with a diminution of its force, in proportion to that of its antagonist. A miracle is a violation of the laws of nature; and as a firm and unalterable experience has established these laws, the proof against a miracle, from the very nature of the fact, is as entire as any argument from experience can possibly be imagined."† Nothing is esteemed a miracle, if it ever happened in the common course of nature. It is no miracle that a man seemingly in good health should die on a sudden; because such a kind of death, though more unusual

---

* Ibid., pp. 91, 92.   † Ibid., p. 93.

than any other, has yet been frequently observed to happen. But it is a miracle, that a dead man should come to life, because that has never been observed* in any age or country. There must, therefore, be a uniform experience against every miraculous event, otherwise the event would not merit that appellation. And as an uniform experience amounts to a proof, there is here a direct and full *proof* from the nature of the fact, against the existence of any miracle, nor can such a proof be destroyed, or the miracle rendered credible, but by an opposite proof, which is superior. The plain consequence is, that no testimony is sufficient to establish a miracle, unless the testimony be of such a kind that its falsehood would be more miraculous than the fact which it endeavors to establish; and even in that case, there is a mutual destruction of arguments, and the superior only gives us an assurance suitable to that degree of force which remains after deducting the inferior.† "It is nothing strange that men should lie in all ages;"‡ so that he affirms that "the knavery and folly of men are such common phenomena, that I should rather believe the most extraordinary events to arise from their concurrence, than admit"§ of a violation of the laws of nature.

---

* Observe how here, in the very midst of his argument, he takes for granted that a miracle has never happened.

† Hume's Essays, as before, Vol. II., pp. 93, 94.

‡ Ibid., p. 97.   § Ibid., p. 106.

He then goes on to allege that no miracle has been found in all history so attested as to secure us from the operation of delusion; that the passions of surprise and wonder arising from miracles, being in themselves agreeable, dispose men to believe them; that miraculous relations chiefly abound among ignorant and barbarous nations; and that such miracles as those alleged to be performed by Vespasian, by St. Francis Assisi, and on the tomb of the Abbè Paris, have been generally discredited; and so, with a pretence of respect for "our most holy religion," which is "founded on faith," and with no examination whatever of the miracles of Christ, he concludes by consigning the Pentateuch and all its miracles to the limbo of lies; and by the sneering paradox, "that the Christian religion not only was at first attended with miracles, but even at this day cannot be believed by any reasonable being without one," since "mere reason is insufficient to convince us of its veracity."*

This argument, as those acquainted with the other writings of its author must well know, has its roots in that philosophy of which he was at once the founder and the expositor. He traced all our knowledge to sensation, so that in his belief nature could be known only through the senses, while he eliminated all notion of power from causation, by defining the relation

---

* Ibid., p. 108.

between cause and effect to be nothing more than that of the invariable sequence of the consequent to the antecedent. In this way neither spirit nor force had any place in the universe as he understood it. He never called himself an atheist, indeed; but if he was a Theist at all, it was after the ancient Epicurean fashion, for his God was only an ornamental appendage to the material system, having as little to do with the origination and government of the world, as the figurehead has had with the building or has with the management of the ship. It is not wonderful, therefore, that with these radical convictions, he denied the possibility of proving miracles; for it is self-evident that no testimony can establish the occurrence of a miracle—not as a violation of a law of nature, for that definition we repudiate, but as a work performed by God out of the usual course of nature—to a man who does not first believe, on independent grounds, that there is a God to perform it. The force of evidence depends not simply on its own clearness and volume, but also on the degree of intelligence possessed, and the nature of the opinions held already by those to whom it is addressed. The inference from one of our Saviour's own parables might have prepared us for such an argument, for He says: "If they believe not Moses and the prophets, neither will they be persuaded though one went unto them from the dead." Miracles and the proof of miracles, were not meant to convince atheists. As we saw in our first lecture, they presuppose and postulate the personal existence and omnipresent agency of God; and we need not be surprised that a philosophy which has no working place for God, though in theory it may still believe in Him, should refuse even to look at the evidence in behalf of miracles.

That I am not wrong in tracing thus Hume's argument against miracles to his Philosophy will be evident from the different disposition shown on this subject, by his great predecessor, John Locke, whose system, erroneous in some respects as it was, still recognised the spiritual nature of man, and the existence and active agency of God. Accordingly, he has written thus:* "Though the common experience and ordinary course of things have justly a mighty influence on the minds of men to make them give or refuse credit to anything proposed to their belief, yet there is one case wherein the strangeness of the fact lessens not the assent to a fair testimony given of it. For when such supernatural events are suitable to ends aimed at by Him who has power to change the course of nature, then under such circumstances they may be fitter to procure belief by how much the more they are beyond or contrary to observation. This is the proper case of miracles, which

---

* "Essay concerning Human Understanding." B. 4, ch. 16, sec. 13.

well attested, do not only find credit themselves, but give it to other truths which need confirmation." Thus a man's philosophy will consciously or unconsciously determine his attitude toward testimony, and so they who hold that there is a spiritual power in man, and that there is a personal God in the universe, will have no difficulty in giving assent to appropriate testimony in behalf of miracles; for the experience of their own power over physical nature will have prepared them to ascribe similar power on fitting occasions to the God of all.

But Hume did not, in so many words, deny the possibility of miracles. He was content with seeking to establish the impossibility of proving that such things had ever occurred. And here, too, those familiar with his writings will understand how he came to take up such a position. For he resolved knowledge into impressions and ideas, or perceived and remembered sensations which might be either lively or faint. This was equivalent to the affirmation that only that which could be perceived through the senses and remembered as having been so perceived could be an object of knowledge. In other words, knowledge in his view is made for us, not by us; and so everything that transcends experience belongs, as being to me neither an impression nor the remembrance of an impression, to the region of the unverifiable or the incredible. Of this psychology, the famous argument of the essay was the legitimate issue. But every one must see that it not only renders miracles incredible, but also makes the accumulation of knowledge, otherwise than by personal experience, impossible. It is, as one has well remarked, "as destructive of science as of religion." But as the same author goes on to say: "If his psychology is denied, his logic is deprived of its premises. If we refuse to recognize man as a series of impressions and ideas, a succession of actual and remembered sensations, he loses the assumption that can alone lend plausibility and force to his argument. If mind creates experience, rather than experience mind, the argument is reversed, the position turned. The only philosophy that can explain knowledge is the philosophy that seeks reason behind and before sensation. Thought is first, not last; is not a product of sensation pure and simple, but the only power that can translate and transmute it into knowledge. But if so, if without the transcendental elements in knowledge the elements furnished by experience are impossible, Hume's elaborate proof of the incredibility of miracles is but a castle in the air, no more consistent than the structure of our dreams."*

Leaving now, however, the principles which are beneath it, let us come to argument itself. We

---

* Dr. A. M. Fairbairn in "The Expositor," Vol. VIII., p. 296.

cannot read it with care without acknowledging its force. Its danger lies in the fact that there is a sense in which the premises are correct, while yet they do not warrant the conclusion which is drawn. We do not deny that experience has established the general uniformity of nature's laws; for if that were not the case, a miracle would not be in any way striking or impressive as a variation from them. Neither do we feel called upon to dispute the assertion that our belief in the testimony of eye-witnesses rests upon our observation of the veracity of human testimony and that in the case of a miracle, the proof furnished by eye-witnesses must be set against the proof for the uniformity of nature's laws, *as far as regards that particular occurrence;* and the conclusion pronounced in favor of that which preponderates. That is precisely the principle on which we go, in our investigation of miracles; and the position which we take up is this, that the testimony of those who give evidence for the miracles of the New Testament is such as not only to counterpoise, but in these instances to outweigh that which is given in behalf of the uniformity of nature's laws.

On Hume's own principle, therefore, as laid down in the earlier extracts we have given from his essay, he ought at once to have gone on to investigate the nature of the testimony borne to these miracles and to see if that did not warrant the belief in their reality, in spite of the experience we have of nature's uniformity. Instead of doing that, however, he has indulged in sundry truisms about human credulity, and then because he finds certain alleged miracles by Vespasian, the Abbè Paris, and St. Francis, unworthy of credence, he rejects those of Christ without deeming the evidence in their behalf worthy of a moment's consideration. But who cares for such alleged miracles as these? They are not on their trial. It was not to undermine belief in them that the famous Essay was written. The whole drift and purpose of the author was to destroy the credibility of the miracles of Christ. Why, then, has he not applied his principle to them? Is there any just ground for doubting the reality of Christ's supernatural works in the facts that false pretensions have been put forth for the Emperor Vespasian, and the Jansenist Abbè? Jesus Christ is not of their company; why, then, should He be condemned simply on their account, and without a trial of His own? "If," says Peter Bayne, "we suppose a man of the highest character put on trial for his life, informed of the law by which he is to be judged; then bidden to stand aside until some one who claims a distant relationship to him, and has no character to plead, is tried in his stead; and lastly, recalled to be told that he is capitally condemned, we shall have no more than faintly shadowed forth the outrageousness of Hume's proceeding."* We do not want to see his principle tested on the wonders on which he expatiates, we want to see him applying it to the miracles of Christ.

But so far from doing that, he has foreclosed the whole matter by a very adroit, and one is almost constrained to add, most perverse and dishonest begging of the question. This is accomplished by the skilful use of the terms "experience" and "testimony," and by the quiet insertion of one unchallenged word in the argument. Let me expose the fallacy. What does he mean by experience, when he says, that it has established the uniformity of nature's laws? If he mean by it his own individual experience, then no objection can be taken to his assertion; but if he mean by it the experience of all men in all ages of the world, then that is taking for granted the thing to be proved, for the very point in dispute is whether the experience of those in the days of Jesus Christ, who declared that they saw His miracles, be not in favor of such supernatural occurrences. This sophism becomes more conspicuous when we look at the word "*unalterable*" which he has prefixed to experience, when he alleges that an "unalterable experience" establishes the laws of nature; for if that ex-

---

* "Testimony of Christ to Christianity," p. 10.

perience is unalterable there is an end of the matter, the subject is foreclosed, and we are sent back to the denial of the possibility of miracles, which we have already exposed. Observe, therefore, how consciously, or unconsciously, I shall not take upon me to determine which, "he falters with the double sense." His argument amounts to this, that because the great mass of mankind have not experienced miracles, therefore we are to set aside altogether the testimony of that portion of the race, who declare in the most credible manner that they saw the miracles of Christ. One is reminded by this of the defence of the Irishman, who on being confronted with a witness who affirmed that he saw him steal, replied, "What of that? I could find a hundred men who could say with truth they didn't!" That we should sift the testimony with the utmost care, we grant. That we should have stronger evidence for a miracle, than for an ordinary event, we are prepared to admit; but that we should be asked on *a priori* grounds to refuse to investigate the evidence advanced in its support, we hold to be inconsistent with that inductive philosophy, one of whose first principles it is that nothing which claims to be a fact, should be rejected without examination.

But this is not all. We have in this argument a comparison of experience with testimony; and a preference is expressed for experience above testimony, as if the two were radically distinct. But, again, we ask, of whose experience does he speak? If it be one's own personal experience, then very clearly that which comes under my own observation makes a more forcible impression on me than that which I learn from the testimony of another. But the question recurs, what has my personal experience to do here? If I had been present when the miracles were wrought, and had observed something different from those who were spectators with me at the time, then my experience might be put against theirs; but as I was not there, nothing that I can say can disprove their statements. It must be, therefore, the general experience of mankind of which Hume speaks, and then the enquiry becomes pertinent, how can we learn what that is except by the very testimony which it is his object to depreciate. Hence, to put the general experience of mankind against testimony, is virtually, after all, only to put testimony against testimony, therefore this famous argument, where it is not a begging of the question, simply throws us back upon the study of the evidence which has been given in support of the miracles and asks us to determine whether it be of such a kind as not only to warrant our belief in their reality, but also to render culpable our unbelief.

Indeed, as we read Hume's Essay in its entirety we can scarcely repress the feeling that its author was conscious, even while writing it, of the inconclusiveness of his reasoning here, for, after all, he virtually abandons his ground. "I own," he says, "there may possibly be miracles or violations of the usual course of nature of such a kind as to admit of a proof from human testimony, though perhaps it will be impossible to find any such in the records of history. Suppose all authors in all languages agree that from the 1st of January, 1600, there was a total darkness over the whole earth for eight days. Suppose that the tradition of this extraordinary event is still strong and lively among the people; that all travellers who return from foreign countries bring us accounts of the same tradition, without the least variation or con tradiction; it is evident that our present philosophers, instead of doubting that fact, ought to receive it for certain, and ought to search for the causes* whence it might be derived." Here, then, on our philosopher's own showing, is a case in which the proof in favor of a miracle, so far from being overborne by the experience of nature's uniformity, is reckoned sufficient to establish the credibility of the occurrence; but the effect of this admission is neutralized and the *animus* of the whole argument revealed by the words

---

* It is curious to see how nature, though expelled with the "fork" of a preconceived philosophy, will return in spite of a man. Hume denies causation in any sense which makes the antecedent produce the consequent, and yet here he speaks of "causes" just as if he held no such theory.

with which he introduces the passage which we have first cited: "I beg the limitations here may be remarked when I say that a miracle can never be proved so as to be the foundation of a system of religion."* And why not? Because "men in all ages have been so much imposed on by ridiculous stories of that kind, that this very circumstance would be a full proof of cheat, and sufficient with all men of sense, not only to make them reject the fact, but even to reject it without examination." To all which we make reply, in the first place, that cases of false miracles, rightly regarded, furnish a proof that there is a legitimate place for true ones. There would be no temptation to the coiner to produce counterfeit money, if there were no such thing as genuine currency. The supply of false miracles, therefore, has been called forth by that principle in the human soul to which true miracles appeal; and impostors never could have succeeded, in any age, if there had not been in man a belief, intuitive or otherwise, in God, coupled with an expectation that any communication which He should make to the human race would be accompanied by supernatural manifestations. And in the second place, we answer, that however credulous men in other ages may have been, such a charge can hardly be legitimately advanced

---

* Essays as before, Vol. II., p. 105.

THE CREDIBILITY OF MIRACLES. 77

against those who lived, and were the leaders of public opinion in the days of Jesus Christ. Morally degraded, indeed, as we have seen they were; but they were intellectually possessed of the highest culture of which the ancient world could boast. Pilate's "what is truth?" does not indicate a credulous, but rather a sceptical mind, and we may not forget that the Sadducees were as likely to suspect and detect imposture, as any of our modern *savants*. Indeed this constant ascription of credulity to the age in which Christianity took its rise is altogether inconsistent with the facts of the case, for wherever credulity and superstition were found by the apostles, these were not the friends, but the enemies of Christianity; and as we see from the cases of Simon Magus, and the Cyprian Elyphas, the Gospel was the means of exposing the deceptions of those who used curious arts, and so of delivering men from their deluding power. Moreover, every scholar must admit the force of Professor Fisher's words when he says: "We have only to remember how Aristotle's writings had been for more than three centuries familiar to educated men; how Thucydides, a century earlier, had illustrated the historical spirit; how Epicureanism, with its bare recognition of the existence of God, united with contempt for the doctrine of a special Providence, was the prevailing philosophy; how Roman law was administered throughout the civilized world; how the philosophical treatises of Cicero exhibit the utter infidelity as to the mythological religion of the statesmen of the time; how a man like Julius Cæsar could avow in the Roman Senate, without protest or contradiction, his disbelief in the existence of the soul after death; how antagonists of Christianity like Lucian and Celsus, treated its claim as to miracles, we have only to remember such facts as these, in order to be assured that the intellectual state of the ancient world was one far removed from childish credulity."*

But while the qualification laid down by Hume against admitting the evidence for a miracle so as to be the foundation of a system of religion, can be thus easily removed, the very fact that he makes such a limitation is an illustration of the spirit by which he was actuated; yet there is no logic in a strong epithet, and I leave you to characterize it for yourselves.

The force of the objections to which this formidable argument is liable, on logical grounds, has been admitted even by Professor Huxley in his recent treatise on the philosophy of Hume, and he has sought to relieve it of its encumbrances by admit-

---

* "Essays on the Supernatural Origin of Christianity," by George P. Fisher, D.D , p. 604.

ting the possibility of the occurrences which have been called miracles, and even the possibility of establishing by good and credible testimony the fact that such occurrences have happened; while he denies that there is, even in them, any proof of supernatural causation. Here are his words: "The day-fly has better grounds for calling a thunder-storm supernatural, than has man, with his experience of an infinitesimal fraction of duration, to say that the most astonishing event that can be imagined is beyond the scope of natural causes,"* and that is only a very rhetorical manner of saying what Baden Powell affirmed, when he said that "no testimony can reach to the supernatural; testimony can apply only to apparent sensible facts; testimony can only prove an extraordinary and perhaps inexplicable occurrence or phenomenon, but (the affirmation) that it is due to supernatural causes is entirely dependent on the previous belief and assumption of the parties."† That is to say, if I am a believer in the personal existence and omnipresent agency of God already, I will refer these occurrences to a supernatural power; but if I deny that there is any God, or any agency in the universe except that which is natural, if with Huxley I believe that nature is "nothing more nor less than

---

* Professor Huxley's "Hume," p. 130.
† "Essays and Reviews," pp. 127, 128.

that which is the totality of events, past, present, and to come,"* I shall regard these events as due to some law which I have not yet discovered.

With this alternative I might well be content to leave the case; but I cannot forbear adding, that if we once admit that the facts as described in the New Testament have occurred, it seems to me that unless we have atheistic preconceptions, we must acknowledge that they were due to the power of God. And the triumphs of our modern scientific men help us to that conclusion, rather than hold us back from it. For, in the discovery of agents formerly unknown in the world, they have come upon none which can give an explanation, on merely natural principles, of the miracles of Christ. It has been alleged indeed that "the inevitable progress of research" must sooner or later unveil the mysteries connected with them all, but we can wait that event with equanimity; and when we reach the day when the tempest can be hushed by some wonder-working philosopher, and the dead raised to life by the command of a leader in some scientific school, we shall be willing to concede the argument, though even then a new miracle would emerge, and the question would become, how do you account for the fact, that Jesus Christ, a young Jewish peasant, should, eighteen hundred years

---

* Huxley's "Hume," p. 129.

ago and without any scientific instructors, have known those secrets of nature, which you have only just discovered?

But, indeed, you cannot explain these Gospel miracles on merely natural principles, without altering the facts, or charging the worker of the miracles, and the witnesses as well, with deception and collusion, and so the easiest, most natural, and most satisfactory account of them is to accept them as works wrought by God, in honor of and for the authentication of His Son, when He sent Him into the world as the Redeemer of the race. And in this last specification you have the answer to the question so often asked by antagonists, Why have we no such things in these days? There were good reasons for miracles then, which do not exist now; for the Son of God was to be heralded to men as such, and in that we find a motive worthy of, and an occasion proper for, the interference with the regular course of nature. But the treatment of this and other similar objections will be more in place in our investigation of the argument of Renan, to which, as given in the Introduction to his Life of Christ, we now proceed.

Here are his words: " None of the miracles with which the old histories are filled took place under scientific conditions. Observation, which has never once been falsified, teaches us that miracles never happen but in times and countries in which they are believed, and before persons disposed to believe them. No miracle ever occurred in the presence of men capable of testing its miraculous character. Neither common people nor men of the world are able to do this. It requires great precautions, and long habits of scientific research. In our days have we not seen almost all respectable people dupes of the grossest frauds, or of puerile illusions? Marvellous facts, attested by the whole population of small towns, have, thanks to a severe scrutiny, been exploded. If it is proved that no contemporary miracle will bear enquiry, is it not probable that the miracles of the past, which have all been performed in popular gatherings, would equally present their share of illusion if it were possible to criticise them in detail? It is not, then, in the name of this or that philosophy, but in the name of universal experience, that we banish miracle from history. We do not say, 'Miracles are impossible.'* We say, 'Up to this time a miracle has never been proved.' If to-morrow a thaumaturgus present himself with credentials sufficiently important to be discussed, and announce himself as able, say, to raise the dead, what would be done? A commission, composed of physiologists, physicists, chemists, persons

---

* Yet in another place he speaks of "the notion of the supernatural with its impossibilities."—See "Life of Jesus," English People's Edition, p. 59.

accustomed to historical criticism would be named. This commission would choose a corpse; would assure itself that death was real; would select the room in which the experiment should be made; would arrange the whole system of precautions, so as to leave no chance of doubt. If, under such conditions, the resurrection were effected, a probability almost equal to certainty would be established. As, however, it ought to be possible always to repeat an experiment —to do over again [that] which has been done once; and as in the order of miracle there can be no question of ease or difficulty, the thaumaturgus would be invited to reproduce his marvellous act under other circumstances, upon other corpses, in another place. If the miracle succeeded each time, two things would be proved: first, that supernatural events happen in the world; second, that the power of producing them belongs, or is delegated to, certain persons. But who does not see that no miracle ever took place under these conditions? but that always hitherto the thaumaturgus has chosen the subject of the experiment, chosen the spot, chosen the public; that, besides, the people themselves—most commonly in consequence of the invincible want to see something divine in great events and great men—create the marvellous legends afterwards? Until a new order of things prevails, we shall maintain, then, this principle of historical criticism, that a supernatural account cannot be admitted as such; that it always implies credulity or imposture; that the duty of the historian is to explain it, and seek to ascertain what share of truth or of error it may conceal."*

There is here, in all the leading features of the argument, an entire identity with that which we have already disposed of; there is the same absence of all reference to the moral element of the question; there is the same appeal to "experience," which is quietly assumed to be "universal;" there is the same insinuation that the miracles of the Gospel stand on a level with modern pretensions to the supernatural, and founded on that, the same refusal even to investigate their claims; while, after all, in the imaginary case that is put before the reader, there is the same virtual abandonment of the principle on which the objection is based; without, however, let us do Renan the justice of adding, the same qualifying imitation which Hume imposed. Still, as there are some specific differences, designed, as it would seem, to adapt the argument to our own days, we may profitably spend a little time in its dissection.

First, let us look at the assertion, that "observation, which has never once been falsified, teaches us that miracles never happen but in times and countries in which they are believed, and before persons dis-

---

* " Life of Jesus," English People's Edition, pp. 29, 30.

THE CREDIBILITY OF MIRACLES. 85

posed to believe them." I do not think that it would be difficult to find instances from among the miracles of the New Testament to which these words would not apply, and perhaps before I finish this investigation I may direct attention to one of the kind; but, meanwhile, I ask you to take notice of the general principle which he designs to insinuate under this apparently harmless statement. He means to convey the idea that a miracle would be more credible to him, and should be more credible to others, if at the time when it was wrought it was disbelieved by those who witnessed it. But is that true? Would not M. Renan himself be the first to reject a miracle which was not attested by the experience of those to whom at first it was submitted? Would he not at once allege, that if those who were present at the time did not believe it, it is preposterous to ask that we should admit its reality? Besides, does not this render it impossible to establish any miracle? For it must either have been believed or rejected by those who were present with the miracle-worker. If it were believed by them, then our author is ready with his assertion, that "miracles are ordinarily the work of the public much more than of him to whom they are attributed;"* if it were not believed by them, then, of course, it would be said that the testimony even

---

* "Life of Jesus," as before, p. 196.

of those who were present conclusively settled that they were spurious. Thus on both sides he is armed. Offer him proof, and he replies, "The witnesses were credulous, and more than half the miracle was in their desire to see it." Tell him that those before whom it was wrought did not receive it, and he will immediately retort, "On what principle am I asked to do what they, with their ampler opportunities for examination, refused to do?" What, then, would he have? and how can he be satisfied? Truly such a spirit as this recalls the Master's words, "Whereunto shall I liken the men of this generation? and to what are they like? They are like children sitting in the market-place, and calling one to another, and saying, We have piped unto you, and ye have not danced; we have mourned unto you, and ye have not wept. But Wisdom is justified of her children."* There must, therefore, be some other course than this if we would follow wisdom.

But it may be said that he has qualified his assertion, inasmuch as in the latter part of the sentence he speaks of the persons not only as having actually believed, but also as having been disposed to believe them; and there is no doubt a wide difference between the two, but the distinction will not help him. For the New Testament contains numerous instances

---

* Luke vii. 31, 32, 35.

THE CREDIBILITY OF MIRACLES. 87

of miracles performed before those who, so far from being disposed to believe them, actually sought out grounds on which to reject them. Of this sort were the opening of the eyes of the man born blind, John ix.; the raising of Lazarus, John xi.; and, as we shall presently make evident, the resurrection of the Lord himself. Now, in the face of these and other similar cases, it is neither just nor reasonable to allege that supernatural works have never been performed, except before persons predisposed in their favor. It is quite possible, indeed, that M. Renan may endeavor to escape from the force of this reply by denying the authenticity of these portions of the sacred books; but admitting that, as he does, when it suits his purpose, we cannot permit him to deny it when the exigencies of argument seem to make it expedient for him to do so. If the Gospels are historic in those portions on which he raises his battering-ram of attack, we should like to see on what distinct principles they are denied to be so in those places where we erect our engines of defence. Such an answer to our reply, therefore, would be to cut the knot, not to loose it.

Further, what does he mean when he declares that "none of the miracles with which old histories are filled took place under scientific conditions?" Is it, indeed, the case, that "neither common people nor men of the world are capable of testing a miracle?"

If the miracles of the Gospels (and it is only those with which these "old histories" are filled that we care to defend) had been wrought alone on substances with which only men of science are familiar, then there might be some show of reason in the assertion; but if they were performed, as they were, in the region of common life, in which the common sense of the multitude is just as sure a guide as the precision of the man of science, then his allegation is most false and fallacious. Take the case, for example, of a dead man raised to life. Rightly here Renan would make the most strict investigation turn on the question, whether or not he had been really dead; but is it true that only a commission* composed of "physicists, physiologists, chemists, and persons accustomed to historical criticism," can decide such a question as that? No doubt the very fact that the person has been raised to life again should, from its unusual occurrence, dispose us to examine minutely into the evidence that he had been really dead; but that is a different thing from

---

* In his demand for such a commission, Renan forestalls that of Mr. Huxley in his work on Hume, "for a monograph by a highly competent investigator." But in his supposed case of the centaur, the Professor restricts himself to an animal appearance, apart from any moral purpose, or the carrying out of any beneficent design, and so fails to recognize the distinction between a prodigy and a miracle. It is not by accident, surely, that all three writers, Hume, Renan, and Huxley, entirely ignore the agency of the individual, at whose word the miracles of the New Testament were performed, and speak merely of spontaneous occurrences.

THE CREDIBILITY OF MIRACLES. 89

saying that we should have a special sort of evidence, differing in kind and not simply in degree, from that which is generally acted on in such cases.

An English judge, some years ago, in a trial which excited universal interest, laid down the principle, that an amount of evidence which would satisfy the jury in acting one way or other in their most important business concerns, would be enough to warrant them in determining the guilt or innocence of the prisoner, even though his life were trembling in the balance; and similarly, an amount of evidence such as would justify us in proceeding to the interment of any member of our family, ought to be sufficient to establish the reality of death in the case of one who has been raised again from the dead.

But perhaps Renan, in demanding this scientific commission, may only wish to determine whether or not the so-called miraculous work was done by the introduction of some natural causes of which the multitude were ignorant, but with which the members of the commission might be familiar. If this be his idea, then we may at once admit that marvellous things do sometimes take place, which careful investigation by competent parties afterwards makes clear; but as we have already asked, in another connection, where is the scientific explanation of the miracles of Christ? The facts are before the world, and have been tested by the science of eighteen hundred years;

yet they have never been accounted for on natural principles, or reproduced by the most eminently scientific men. If, therefore, science has detected other impositions, how have these, supposing them to be impositions, eluded her vigilance? Is it not because they lie in a region beyond her ken? The line which divides the natural from the supernatural is not always very easily defined. Yet in this instance we do not need science to make it clear; for, in the words of another: "The great bulk of the miracles of Scripture are distinguished from common events by so broad a line, that if we admit the fact of their occurrence, we cannot, with any reason, question their miraculous character. Besides, we must not overlook that the miracles of Scripture took place not spontaneously, but at the command of some individual man. A human mouth speaks, and the blind see, the deaf hear, the rigid joint relaxes. Christ says, 'Lazarus, come forth,' and the dead man stands alive before him. To allow such facts, and yet to say that they may have sprung from natural causes, is to concede to Christ a mastery over nature's secrets unequalled since the world began; which, if he were a mere man, and his religion a fable, is not less miraculous than all the miracles recorded in Scripture.*

---

* "The Miracles of Scripture defended from the Assaults of Modern Scepticism," by William Lindsay, D.D., pp. 26, 27.

Nor is this all: are scientific men, such as "physiologists, physicists, and chemists," not just as liable to be imposed upon as others? We apprehend it would not be difficult to bring together a list of instances in which the credulity of many modern "*savants*" would appear in a most ridiculous light, as showing that their prepossessions and prejudices very largely affect their conclusions, and make them act in some cases in a manner altogether inconsistent with just principles of "historical criticism." Besides, where is the question on which scientific men will not be found ranged on either side, uttering the most opposite things? Let any one throw himself back upon the records of important trials in our own land for the last ten years, and think of the conflicting statements in relation to poisons and insanity which have been put forth by one class of men of science among us, and if after that he be disposed to place implicit faith in a commission of "chemists and physicists," we shall be greatly surprised. There are subjects which the mass of the people understand, to say the least, as well as men of science, and on which the judgment of the community, howsoever it may be arrived at, is more reliable than theirs.* In say-

---

* Christlieb reminds us that the French Academy rejected the use of quinine, vaccination, lightning-conductors; the existence of meteorolites, and the steam-engine. See "Modern Doubt and Christian Belief," p. 324.

ing this, I mean no disrespect to the great body of earnest and philosophic thinkers who are numbered among our men of science; I only allege that they have not a monopoly of common sense, to the utter exclusion of the "common people and the men of the world."

But leaving these assertions, let us look at the evidence in behalf of one of our Lord's miracles, and see if we have not an amount of proof which, judging from the case which He has put before us, ought to satisfy even M. Renan. We say *ought* to satisfy him, for after all we feel persuaded that if every condition prescribed by himself were complied with to the very letter, he would yet contrive to evade the conclusions which he seems to admit would in that case be logically deducible.

Still, that we may show that even on Renan's own ground the evidence is satisfactory, let us take the miracle of our Lord's resurrection, and see if in the main it do not satisfy all his "scientific conditions."

In the first place, the disciples were not looking for His resurrection, neither were they *à priori* disposed to believe it;* for though Jesus himself had repeatedly referred to it in His intercourse with them, they had at the time misunderstood His meaning, and they had afterwards forgotten His words. Nothing seems

---

* Luke xxiv. 11

more clear on the face of the record than that the resurrection took the disciples by surprise; hence they had no prepossession in favor of believing it, and so on this point they are witnesses according to Renan's own heart.

Again, Christ was really dead. This is admitted by Renan himself, who gives an account of the crucifixion scene, and ends with a strange rhapsodical apostrophe to Jesus. But in order to show that even no man of science need have doubt on this point, we may simply recall the facts, that the soldiers, accustomed to look on death, and who therefore knew it when they saw it, did not break the legs of Jesus, for they perceived He was dead already; and that one of them, to make assurance doubly sure, " with a spear pierced His side, and forthwith came thereout blood and water."* Now, strangely enough, a scientific commission, so to speak, though at the distance of eighteen centuries, has sat upon this occurrence, and has given a decision on it to the effect that death was not caused by the spearthrust, but that the blood and water which flowed from the wound showed that a very short while before, Jesus had died of a broken heart.† About

---

* John xix. 34.
† See this subject very fully treated by Dr. Hanna in his "Last Day of our Lord's Passion," pp. 290, etc. ; see also the appendix to the same work, where the opinion of Dr. Stroud is corroborated by that of Drs. Begbie, Simpson, and Struthers.

the reality of His death, therefore, there can be no dispute.

Next let us look at the sepulchre. This, as we know, was not a place chosen by those who wished to have it as the best possible "in which the experiment should be made," but virtually it was all that any scientific commission could have desired, for it was a new tomb, in which no body had ever been laid, and where, therefore, there was no possibility of substituting one corpse for another; besides this, it was closely secured by the stone and seal, and strictly watched by the guard of soldiers. Here, therefore, great precautions were exercised; but how utterly useless they all were!

> "Hell and the grave combined their force
> To hold our Lord in vain;
> Sudden the Conqueror arose,
> And burst their feeble chain."

In proof of this resurrection we appeal to the testimony of those who saw Him "alive after His passion," and who had no motive for saying other than the truth. He was really dead; they saw Him afterwards alive, with such marks of identity as made it clear to them that it was He. Can any evidence be better? To all this, however, M. Renan only says, "Such was the impression He had left in the hearts of His disciples, and of a few devoted women, that during some weeks more it was as if He were living and consoling them. Had His body been taken away? or did enthusiasm, always credulous, create afterwards the group of narratives by which it was sought to establish faith in His resurrection? In the absence of opposing documents, this can never be ascertained. Let us say, however, that the strong imagination of Mary Magdalene played an important part in this circumstance. Divine power of love, sacred moments in which the passion of a possessed woman gives to the world a resuscitated God."* Verily the man who can believe that, need not object to miracles on the score of their incredibility.

But we cannot allow M. Renan thus to trample underfoot the laws of historic evidence; and we insist that if the Gospels be accepted on such matters as he receives, they be regarded also as at least credible statements of what the witnesses themselves have said on other points. Now, we find that not "the imagination of Mary Magdalene" only, but the sober sense of John and Peter, the observation of the ten apostles in the upper room, and the very scepticism of Thomas which was so thoroughly removed, all go together to establish the fact of the Saviour's reäppearance. Nor was it only an impression of weeks; for Paul, writing at least thirty years after the event, could say, "He was seen of about five hundred breth-

---

* "Life of Jesus," English Translation as before, p. 296.

ren at once, of whom the greater part remain unto this present, but some have fallen asleep; last of all, He was seen of me also."* Here, then, we have a miracle which took the disciples by surprise, and was performed as nearly as possible under scientific conditions. All that is needed to complete Renan's requirements is its repetition again and again; but as the resurrection of Christ was itself the fourth miracle of the kind which Jesus wrought, each one ascending above the other in regular gradation up to this last and crowning one, we may hold that even that is satisfied, and press him to the admission of his two conclusions: first, that supernatural events happen in the world; and second, that the power of producing them belongs or is delegated to certain persons. Without waiting for any "new order of things to prevail,"† therefore, we insist on it that he abandon the principle that a supernatural event cannot be admitted as such, but always implies either credulity or imposture; and over against his treatment of the miracles and resurrection of Christ, we take leave to

---

* 1 Cor. xv. 6, 8.

† We cannot see, indeed, how Renan needs thus to qualify his words, for on his principle how is a "new order of things" to be introduced? how are men to prove it when it comes? and how, without credulity, is it to be acknowledged as real? The phrase, however, is valuable, as revealing that in a moment of unconsciousness, he, like Hume, in the passage noticed on a previous page, returns to the common modes of expression, and the recognition of the truths that lie beneath them.

place the statement of one of whose name and fame England is justly proud, and who is entitled in this department to be heard with deference. Dr. Arnold, of Rugby, in one of those sermons to the "boys," which are so full of manliness and true Christian nobleness, has said: "The evidence of our Lord's life and death and resurrection may be, and often has been, shown to be satisfactory; it is good according to the common rules for distinguishing good evidence from bad. Thousands and tens of thousands of persons have gone through it piece by piece as carefully as ever judge summed up on a most important cause. I have myself done it many times over, not to persuade others, but to satisfy myself. I have been used for many years to study the history of other times, and to examine and weigh the evidence of those who have written about them, and *I know of no one fact in the history of mankind which is proved by better and fuller evidence of every sort, to the understanding of a fair inquirer, than the great sign which God hath given us that Christ died and rose again from the dead.*"*

---

* "Sermons on Christian Life," pp. 15, 16.

THE TESTIMONY
IN BEHALF OF MIRACLES.

LECTURE IV.

THE TESTIMONY IN BEHALF OF MIRACLES.

John viii. 18 : I am one that bear witness of myself.
2 Peter i. 16 : We were eye-witnesses of His majesty.

HAVING fought our way through the barriers which have been raised by some, to prevent even an investigation of the miracles of the New Testament, we are now prepared to examine the evidence by which they are attested. For this purpose we must betake ourselves to the Gospel narratives themselves; nor let any one imagine that in following this course, we are acting in a manner that is either unwarranted or illogical, for we are not now taking for granted the divine authority of these documents. We are, as in the outset I was careful to show, dealing thus far only with their credibility; but even for the settlement of that, it is indispensable that we look to the statements which they contain. These books are the depositions of the witnesses, and as in a court of justice it is impossible to judge of the credibility of those who give evidence, apart from the evidence which they give, so we cannot hope to arrive at any right conclusion as to the worth of this testimony without examining it; only let it be understood that in making such an investigation, we shall treat it simply as an ordinary production, and build nothing upon that inspiration, with which, in the estimation of all Christians, its authors were endowed.

Now, the first witness whom we call, is Jesus Christ himself. It is undeniable that He himself laid claim to the possession of supernatural power. Thus, when the disciples of John the Baptist came to Him in their master's name to ask: "Art thou he that should come, or do we look for another?" He answered: "Go and show John again those things which ye do hear and see: the blind receive their sight and the lame walk; the lepers are cleansed, and the deaf hear; the dead are raised up, and the poor have the Gospel preached to them."* Again, to the Jews, He said: "I have greater witness than that of John; for the works which the Father hath given me to finish, the same works that I do, bear witness of me, that the Father hath sent me."† On another occasion, He expressed Himself thus: "If I do not the work of my Father, believe me not. But if I do, though ye believe not me, believe the works: that ye may know and believe that the Father is in me, and I in Him."‡ To the same

---

* Matt. xi. 3, 4, 5. Luke vii. 19–23.
† John v. 36.   ‡ John x. 37, 38.

effect is His language to Philip: "Believe me that I am in the Father, and the Father in me, or else believe me for the very works' sake."* And, to mention only one saying more, when summing up the guilt of the men of His generation, He spake in this wise: "If I had not done among them the works which none other man did, they had not had sin; but now have they both seen and hated, both me and my Father."† Now we may fairly ask if such an one, as all through these narratives He is represented to be, would make such a claim, if it were ill-founded and untrue? Here are clear and repeated affirmations on the part of Jesus himself that He did work miracles; and the question is, can we believe HIM? In answer to that enquiry, all that I have already advanced for another purpose, in my second lecture, would be equally pertinent here. I might dwell on the moral majesty of His character, as it reveals itself to us through the holy simplicity of these four gospels; and then I might ask whether the falsehood of the testimony of such a witness would not be a greater miracle, even than the raising of the dead to life? But to prevent repetition, I content myself with this reference to that former argument, and proceed to look at the matter from another angle.

It is admitted by all, then, that the evidence of

---

*John xiv. 11.   † John xvi. 24.

Jesus Christ is more than usually valuable in every respect, except when it bears witness to the supernatural in His person and in His works. Even those who repudiate the claims that are now under discussion, will concede that. I have but to remind you of the quotations which I have already made from Lecky and Mill, in this regard; and of such words as these, which form the conclusion of Renan's chapter on the crucifixion: "Thou wilt become to such a degree the corner-stone of humanity, that to tear thy name from this world would be to shake it to its foundations. Between thee and God, men will no longer distinguish,"* to convince you that my representation is correct. Indeed, so high is the estimate of the trustworthiness of Jesus, that but for their pre-judgment of the impossibility of the supernatural, there would have been no disposition on the part of these writers to question His integrity in any respect. Now we may put the case thus: Which is the more reasonable, that the pre-supposition that makes miracles impossible is wrong, or that such a witness as the Lord Jesus Christ is acknowledged to be, was guilty of imposture, or the victim of delusion? We are continually taunted by our modern philosophers with preferring theology to science; and it is supposed that our prejudices unfit us for rightly estimating scientific evi-

---

* Renan, "Life of Jesus," as before, p. 291.

dence: but may we not here fairly retort that the opponents of the miracles are allowing their ante-supernatural prepossessions to unfit them for the right interpretation of moral evidence? One thing, at least, is clear, we cannot consistently reject this testimony without impugning either the moral truthfulness or the intellectual soundness of Jesus Christ; and the moment we do that, we raise these questions, which are harder to solve by far than it is to believe in a miracle; namely: how came the purest morality the world has ever seen from the heart of one who was himself a deceiver? or how came the healthiest, wholesomest, and most intellectually quickening religion with which men are acquainted, from the soul of one who was himself a weak-minded and deluded fanatic? We accept Hume's law here, and boldly affirm that the testimony of Jesus to His own miracles is of such a kind that its falsehood would be more miraculous than the facts which it endeavors to establish; nay, that if such testimony is to be set aside, it will be utterly impossible to establish anything by means of human evidence.

Look at the alternatives for a moment or two. Jesus was either a deceiver, wilfully leading others astray; a victim of hallucination, leading men after phantoms, which yet He believed to be truths; or endowed with moral honesty, and mental soundness. Now which of these can we accept?

Was He a deceiver? Those who answer this question in the affirmative commonly allege, that as the Messiah, whose advent was anticipated by the Jews, was expected to be a worker of miracles, it was quite to be supposed that Jesus, in laying claim to be received as the Christ, should make pretensions to the exercise of supernatural power. They allege that He could not have hoped for success, without conforming, in this respect, to the expectations of the people; and that, even if it did not form a part of His original plan, He was, in a manner, forced to assume the character of a worker of miracles.

But this theory fails to take account of two things: the one in Christ himself, and the other in the Jews of His time. It loses sight of the fact, that from first to last, Jesus was more concerned with truth, than with popularity or success. He did nothing for immediate effect. He never pandered to the wishes of the multitude, or adjusted His sails to the prevailing breeze. He would not even work miracles to satisfy a vain curiosity, or for merely sensational purposes. His standard of action was the right; and He was always more concerned to speak the truth than to swell the number of His followers. He never enticed any one to follow Him on false pretences. He never sought to gain adherents by dazzling their eyes with bright visions of unbroken ease. To the impulsive man who cried to Him in a fit of momentary enthusiasm, "Lord,

TESTIMONY IN BEHALF OF MIRACLES. 107

I will follow Thee, whithersoever Thou goeth," He said: "Foxes have holes, and birds of the air have nests, but the Son of man hath not where to lay His head."* He laid down the law of discipleship to all enquirers, thus: "If any man will come after me, let him deny himself, and take up his cross daily, and follow me."† He desired all who joined Him to "count the cost"‡ of allegiance to Him, lest, meeting unexpected difficulties, they should be discouraged, and turn back. Now if He was thus frank, candid, and honest, with enquirers when they came to Him, is it consistent with probability, I might, indeed, almost say, with possibility, that when He went to them, He was so eager to win their homage as the Messiah, that He stooped to deceive them with magical tricks which He called miracles? He did not care enough for popularity to angle for followers by telling them lies as to what should be their experience as His disciples; but He did care enough for it to pander to the appetite for miracles, by professing to perform supernatural works, which, however, were only pretended miracles, good enough as feats of legerdemain, but really lies, as He employed them. It is a psychological impossibility that both of these can be true; and, seeing as I do, that all through His history, Jesus followed the truth, careless whether or not the crowd followed Him,

---

*Luke ix. 57, 58. † Luke ix. 23. ‡ Luke xiv. 25–33.

I hold that it is harder to believe the falsehood of His testimony to His own miracles, than it is to believe in one of these miracles themselves.

But further, the notion that Jesus was a deceiver, takes no account of the fact, well known to every student, that in the time of His appearance, the Jewish ideal of what their Messiah was to be, was entirely different from the reality which He presented. I admit, indeed, that His person, life, and work, were fulfilments of Old Testament prophecies; but then they were fulfilments which gave, for the first time, their true interpretations to these prophecies; for here, as so often in the providence of God, it was the unexpected that happened, and Jesus came in such a way as to prove that He was the Messiah; but, also, in such a way, as to make manifest that the notions prevailing among the people, as to what the Messiah was to be, were grossly one-sided, and therefore false. They expected Him to be a temporal prince, and hoped that He would work out for them a great deliverance from that foreign dominion under which they felt themselves so humiliated. Looking now at the prophecies, in the light of that which we believe to be their fulfilment, we are surprised that they should have formed such erroneous expectations regarding the person and work of their Messiah. But the fact that they did so is undeniable. Even the disciples of Jesus themselves nursed, to the very last moment of their visible fellowship with Him, the fond anticipation that He would restore the kingdom to Israel,* and repeatedly the same view regarding the mission of the Messiah was expressed by the common people in their intercourse with Him. On one occasion, indeed, after the performance of one of the miracles of the loaves and fishes, the multitude, roused to a pitch of enthusiasm, were for taking Him by force and making Him a king. All that was needed, apparently, to His immediate acceptance with them was the proclamation of His earthly royalty. Still He refused to yield to their desire; and because He would not be the king they wished, "from that time many of His disciples went back and walked no more with Him."† Now see what an absurdity this one scene involves, if we must write down Jesus as a deceiver. In order to find acceptance with the people as their Messiah, He wrought what looked like a miracle, but was not really one, to feed them; but when that *ruse* succeeded, and they were on the point of proclaiming Him to be the Messianic king, He distinctly disclaimed their idea of His royalty, and turned multitudes away from Him. If He yielded to their preconceived opinions on the point of the miracles, why did He not yield to them also in the matter of the royalty? And if He refused to conform to their pre-

---

* Acts i. 6. † John vi. 15–60.

possessions, in the affair of the kingship, when His doing so was all that was needed to float Him into success, is it conceivable that, as regards the miracles, He should have made a claim which He knew to be false, simply with the view of suiting Himself to the ideas of the multitude? The law which the impostor must follow, is that which the poet has laid down for the actor, this, namely: "Who live to please, must please to live;" and had there been nothing better in Jesus than the adroitness of a deceiver, He would undoubtedly have yielded to the pressure of the populace, and raised the standard of a new royalty in the land. But that He so solemnly and steadily resisted their importunity on this head, clearly shows that He had some nobler principle to guide Him than the love of popular applause, and makes untenable the view of those who hold that He was, in a manner, forced to pretend to work miracles, in order to secure the favor of the people.

Whether, therefore, we look at the honesty of Jesus, as it comes out in respect to things wherein the supernatural element is not involved, or at the independence with which, in other matters, He steered His course in the very teeth of popular prejudice, it is impossible to rest in the idea that He sought to deceive men by false miracles; and when to these considerations we add that of the moral incongruities involved in the very idea of His being a deceiver, as these were described in a former lecture, we shall see reason to conclude, either that Jesus rightly and truthfully laid claim to the performance of miracles, or that He must no longer be regarded as a pattern of moral excellence, but rather as one of the basest of men, since in Him the practices of the deceiver were united to the clearest perceptions of the right, the true, and the good. If we admit the claim to the supernatural to be well founded, then we have an entirely homogeneous character in Jesus, and everything in it is harmonious with all the rest; but if we deny that claim, then we have in Him a moral anomaly which is more inconceivable in the department of humanity, than a miracle is in that of physical nature; and having proved before that a miracle is possible, we may surely now draw the inference, that if such an one as Jesus was, did actually declare that He performed miracles, it is far more consistent with right reason to suppose that He was speaking the truth, even though that should imply the occurrence of something out of the usual course of nature, than it is to believe that He was uttering a deliberate and predetermined lie. "I believe," with Mr. Bayne, "that the word of one true man is surer evidence than the experience of nature's uniformity for a thousand years; and that the spiritual philosophy which accords this supremacy to the deliberate accents of reason and conscience, which owns the majesty of man, as transcending the authority of nature, is infinitely more profound than the philosophy of Hume."*

But if we can find no sure means of overturning the testimony of Jesus by adopting the theory that He was a deceiver, is the case any better when we try the hypothesis of delusion? Was He a visionary enthusiast, who believed Himself to possess a power which He really had not? We concede at once here that many such individuals have appeared at different times among men; but, of them all it may be affirmed that they were deficient in intellectual balance, or wanting in moral principle, or that both of these characteristics belonged to them. We have already tested the hypothesis of deceit in its reference to Jesus; we have now, therefore, to ask whether He had any mental peculiarity which rendered it probable or conceivable that He should believe Himself to be what He really was not?

It would not be possible, in an argument so condensed as that which I am prosecuting, to enter upon an exhaustive analysis of the intellectual powers of Jesus, as these come out before us in the Gospels. I may simply say that no one can read these records without coming to the conclusions that the mind of Christ was pre-eminently a healthy one, and that His intellect was admirably balanced. There is no evi-

---

* "Testimony of Christ to Christianity," by Peter Bayne, p. 8.

dence of the existence in Him of a morbid exaggeration of any faculty to the detriment of the rest. The speculative in Him did not destroy the practical, neither did the practical interfere with the speculative. His mind as it is here presented to us is full-orbed. In other men, no matter how great they are in some respects, we discover that they are signally defective in others; but, in Jesus, we have "the vision of the faculty divine" by which the poet is distinguished, and, along with that, the philosophic insight in its clearest manifestation; while at the same time we have the sagacity and shrewd common-sense of a practical man of the world.

There is in Him a wonderful "harmony of opposites," and we cannot peruse the accounts of His treatment of the different classes of men with whom He came into contact without having the conviction forced upon us that He was no crazy fanatic, or hairbrained and deluded enthusiast. In point of intellectual ability He must be placed above Zeno, or Socrates, or Plato, or Aristotle; and, in the matter of practical wisdom, not one even of these may be compared with Him. He is as far removed as possible from the mere one-sided man. He looks all round every subject, and sees with unerring precision and at once the principle by which it is to be settled. He is never carried away by impulse or moved by caprice, but His emotions rise out of His judgment and are as sound as their source. Even those who cavil at His system and refuse to receive it entire, are forward to confess all this. Renan has himself said that "His admirable good sense guided Him with marvellous certainty;" that "His leading quality was an infinite delicacy;" and that "He laid with rare forethought the foundations of a Church destined to endure."*

Now, we may safely ask, if such a man—judging Him at present by no higher than a human standard—was likely to become the victim of hallucinations, and so to believe himself to have a power which He did not really possess? Recollect that the narratives which declare that He claimed to work miracles do at the same time make manifest that He possessed what one has called "the most clear, balanced, serene, and comprehensive intellect known to history;"† and then the dilemma appears as before. Either we must receive this description of His intellectual character, and along with that acknowledge the truthfulness of His claim to supernatural power, or, if we hold that though His miracles were false, He sincerely believed that He could and did work real miracles, then we must reject the account which has been given us of His mental greatness. We cannot hold by both.

* "Life of Jesus," as before, pp. 108, 207, 209.
† Bayne's "Testimony of Christ to Christianity," p. 79.

The history which records the claim of Jesus to work miracles is at the same time full of illustrations of His intellectual ability, and the two things are in absolute harmony as we find them there, so that the choice comes to be between rejecting His character as a whole and receiving it as a whole. We cannot accept His intellectual pre-eminence and believe in His hallucination; we cannot believe in His hallucination and accept His intellectual pre-eminence. The choice is here again between the acceptance and rejection of the narrative as a whole. We must either cease to admire Jesus, or bow down and worship Christ; and with that statement we leave this section of the argument, sure what the verdict of a thoughtful man must be; for the Jesus of the Gospels will not lightly be let go by any one who loves the true, the beautiful, and the good.

But we call now the apostles to give their testimony; and, in considering what they have to say, there are two preliminary facts which must be taken into account:

1. *They had perfect opportunities for investigating the wondrous works to which they gave testimony.* The miracles of Jesus were not wrought in secret; they were not "done in a corner," neither did they require darkness for their performance; but they were wrought in open day, before enemies and friends

alike, and the fullest opportunity of exposing them, if they were forgeries, was given to the world. On one or two occasions, indeed, none but the three favored disciples were present; but even then we have every word established in the mouth of two or three witnesses; and at all other times there was the most open and undisguised procedure. The daughter of Jairus was raised to life, in spite of the mocking scorn of those who were perfectly convinced that she was dead; and though the scoffers were excluded from the chamber, the father and the mother of the maiden, and the "first three" of the apostles were present with him at the time. The widow's son was recalled to life at the gate of Nain, the place of public concourse, and in the presence of all who bore the bier and followed it; and Lazarus was brought out of the sepulchre before a promiscuous assemblage of individuals, who had come from Jerusalem to comfort his sorrowing sisters.

So with the rest of His miracles. What could be more public than His feeding of the multitude upon the mountain-side? what more unconcealed than His healing of the blind man at the gate of Jericho? Nor must it be alleged that all these things were done only before His friends, who were willing to believe anything about Him; for, even at the raising of Lazarus, there were some present, who, while unable to deny the miracle, were yet so full of enmity toward Him, that they went and told the Pharisees; and when the blind man was healed at the gate of the temple, there was a judicial investigation into the case by the rulers of the people. Let any one read the ninth chapter of John's Gospel, and he will be able to judge whether it is likely that the men who could use such means as the rulers employed on that occasion, and were filled with such bitter hatred toward Jesus as then they manifested, would leave His other miracles unsifted. Whatever else may be said, therefore, about the miraculous works of Jesus, it cannot with truth be alleged that they were done in secret, or that no proper opportunity of inquiring into them was furnished to the world. Now, this is of the greatest importance, from its bearing on the value of the testimony given by His followers; for there was the fullest opportunity for investigation, and no one can object to their evidence on the ground that they were denied the means of examining into the character of the works of their Master.

2. *They were competent to judge of them.* On this point I have already remarked, when replying to Renan's demand for miracles under "scientific conditions," and it may be sufficient simply to remind you of what I then advanced. Had the works of Jesus been performed on substances with which the disciples were not familiar; had they borne any resemblance to the experiments of the laboratory; or

had He in working them used any material agent with whose properties they were not perfectly acquainted —then their testimony, however valuable it might have been in establishing the fact that Christ did the wonders, would yet have been insufficient to prove that these wonders were true miracles. But instead of this He employs means which are perfectly within the sphere of their knowledge, and produces effects entirely beyond anything which these means themselves would accomplish, so that the proof of a miracle is plain and conclusive. Thus, every man knows quite well what a human touch can do, and what is beyond its power. It does not require a college of philosophers to inform us on that matter, for here one man knows quite as much as another; but Jesus by a touch cleansed the leper, opened the eyes of the blind, and unstopped the ears of the deaf; and hence, when He did so, there was a miracle, on which every man of ordinary discernment is competent to pronounce an opinion. So also we know as much of the properties of dust and the human spittle, as to convince us that, in itself considered, the clay formed by the mixture of the two will be in ordinary circumstances useless as an eye-salve. No medical man, with the least hope of success, would ever employ such a remedy; yet in the case of a man born blind, and well known in the neighborhood, we have the anointing of his eyes with this preparation, and the washing of it off in a certain pool, the means of producing a perfect cure. Let these facts, as simple facts, be but well authenticated, and one man is just as good a judge as another of their miraculous character. But to authenticate them we do not require any more than the average intelligence and common sense of men ; so that we must not reject the testimony of the disciples, on the allegation that they were incompetent to examine the miracles, and pronounce upon them.

Now, that the disciples do give testimony to these facts, is patent to every one who reads their narratives. This is, indeed, the reason why very many reject their writings; but on what ground is this rejection based? If we cannot believe them, then in their case, as in their Master's, we have a choice between these two alternatives—either they were the victims of their own credulity, or they were themselves practicing on the credulity of others. In plain Saxon phrase, they were either fools or knaves, if they were not trustworthy witnesses.

Can they reasonably be supposed to have been the victims of their own credulity? We have seen that no secrecy was attempted by Jesus, and that the works themselves were wrought in the plane of their knowledge, and therefore that they were thoroughly competent to judge regarding them—as much so, indeed, as any common jury among ourselves is to deal with the evidence which is generally submitted to them.

Now, with these preliminaries conceded—and I see not how they can be denied—it follows that if the disciples were deceived, they must have been the veriest simpletons. But does this accord with the description that is given of their mental endowments? I grant, indeed, that the majority of them were plain, blunt men, of little education, and with no great social position; but we cannot harmonize their character in other respects with the idea that they were such imbeciles as to be easily duped by the pretences of an impostor. They had practical sagacity of the soundest kind; and, as their writings show, they were possessed of intellectual ability of no mean order. Take Peter, for example, and what force of character appears in him! Read his Epistles, and you will be struck with the wisdom of his counsels and the thoughtfulness of his words; and as you peruse the opening chapters of the Acts of the Apostles, you will not be able to help admiring the earnestness, the acuteness, the power of debate, and skill in the management of difficult matters which he displays. Plainly this is not the type of a man who is easily imposed upon. Let him be what he may, he is no fool. There are in him soundness of judgment and clearness of intellectual perception, coupled with an outspoken honesty of nature which would have revolted against anything like systematic fraud. True, he denied his Lord in the palace of the high-priest; but that was under pressure of momentary temptation, and was out of keeping with his entire life, while the bitterness of his after weeping, and the character of his subsequent history, betoken how deeply he repented of his sin. Now this man gives no uncertain testimony on the point before us. Again and again he appeals to the miracles which Jesus did before the multitude, and declares that he was "a man approved of God among them by miracles, and signs, and wonders, which God did by him in the midst of them."* Nor is this all; when writing in his old age a letter, which might be valued by men after his decease, he reiterates his assertion, saying, "We have not followed cunningly-devised fables, but were eye-witnesses of his majesty."† Now, we ask, is it likely that a man of this mould could be so imposed upon by a pretender, that he should adhere thus pertinaciously to the witness which he gives?

But there were others among the disciples with distinctive characteristics as inconsistent with the supposition that they were deceived as any which Peter possessed. What shall we say of such an one as Thomas? Here was a man who would accept of no testimony save that of his own senses, and who would sift for himself every matter to the bottom. Whatever others might be disposed to do, he would not receive anything save on his own personal experi-

---

* Acts ii. 22.   † 2 Peter i. 16.

ence; yet even he was satisfied, and constrained to cry out, "My Lord, and my God!"

There was Philip, too, who, as is evident from his interruption of the valedictory discourse, "Lord, show us the Father, and it sufficeth us,"* had very much in common with Thomas, and was possessed of an inquisitive mind, not easily satisfied, and not willing to rest in that which he did not clearly comprehend.

There was also the author of the fourth gospel, who was very far from being intellectually incapable; so far, indeed, that the record he has given taxes the highest minds of our age to understand it, for all so simple as at first it looks. No one can thoughtfully read his pages without seeing the stamp of reality on every one of them, and feeling that he spoke no words of course, but the plain unvarnished truth, when he said in his Epistle, "That which we have seen with our eyes, which we have looked upon, and our hands have handled, of the Word of life; that which we have seen and heard, declare we unto you."†

Of the other apostles and disciples (with the exception of Paul, who comes behind as one "born out of due time,") there are too few personal traits given us to enable us to speak with precision regarding them; but surely, concerning those to whom we have referred, there is no plausible ground for maintaining

---

* John xiv. 8.   † 1 John i. 3.

the idea that they were deluded simpletons, the victims of a designing impostor. Take their intellectual ability as evinced not only in their writings, but in the effects produced by them upon their age, and then view, in connection with that, the considerations already presented as to the opportunities afforded them for investigation, and the knowledge required to enable them to come to a decision on the subject, and we arrive at but one conclusion—namely, that these men cannot be viewed as the blindly credulous followers of one by whom they were cunningly deluded.

There remains the other horn of the dilemma, Were they themselves deceivers? Now here, as in the case of their Master, there are moral considerations which render it utterly impossible for us to think them guilty of such baseness. In the first place, there is the uniform good character which they bore. Even their enemies give testimony to the rectitude and blamelessness of their lives. They stood out from among those by whom they were surrounded, as men of truth and purity and excellence. They were not brought before the judges for "matters of wrong or wicked lewdness;" they were simple in manners, pure in speech, holy in behavior, and there was found "no occasion against them, except it were in the matter" of their Lord. The well-known letter of Pliny to the Emperor Trajan gives an account of the mode of life of the early Christians generally, at the close of the first century. But of these excellent ones the apostles were the leaders and the best; and if they were impostors, we are asked to believe that a system which even its enemies declare to be the purest the world has ever seen, was founded, and conduct which even their persecutors declared to be irreproachable, was practiced, by men who yet were systematically and deliberately propagating a lie. We have no words strong enough to express the revulsion with which we would turn from such a man as Peter, if, after his exposure of the sin of Ananias, such a course could be pursued by him. But it cannot be: the prickly thistle of deceit never yet produced the mellow berries and rich grape clusters of the vine, and never from such a lying root could the fair tree of gospel morality have sprung.

Besides, what conceivable motive could they have had for persevering in this course of deception? From the time of Pentecost forward, all their ideas of earthly glory were abandoned, and they became convinced that the kingdom of Jesus was "not of this world;" yet from that same date their testimony was of the clearest and most unwavering character. Not riches, nor honor, nor power, nor glory, in a worldly sense, could they expect; but instead, persecution, reproach, and a violent death. Yet "none of these things moved them;" but they "took joyfully the spoiling of their goods," and "counted not their lives dear unto them," that they might be Christ's witnesses wherever they went.

Nor is this all: among such a company of deceivers, if they were deceivers, it is inconceivable that no one of them should have turned against the rest, and sought his personal safety by bringing their trickery to view; yet that was never done. The nearest approach to anything of the kind was in the case of Judas; but as one has very quaintly said, " He was so struck with remorse at the thought of giving up his lies and becoming an honest man, that he went and hanged himself."* On the whole, then, we may sum up this part of the argument in the words of Dr. Hill: " The history of mankind has not preserved a testimony so complete and satisfactory as that which I have now stated. If, in conformity to the exhibitions which these writings give of their character, you suppose their testimony to be true, then you can give the most natural account of every part of their conduct— of their conversion, their steadfastness, their heroism. But if, notwithstanding every appearance of truth, you suppose their testimony to be false, inexplicable circumstances of glaring absurdity crowd upon you. You must suppose that twelve men of mean birth, of no education, living in that humble station which

---

* Lecture of Wm. Lindsay, D.D., as before. p. 30.

placed ambitious views out of their reach and far from their thoughts, without any aid from the State, formed the noblest scheme that ever entered into the mind of man, adopted the most daring means of executing that scheme, and conducted it with such address as to conceal the imposture under the semblance of simplicity and virtue. You must suppose that men guilty of blasphemy and falsehood, united in an attempt the best contrived, and which has in fact proved the most successful for making the world virtuous; that they formed this singular enterprise without seeking any advantage to themselves, with an avowed contempt of honor and profit, and with the certain expectation of scorn and persecution; that although conscious of one another's villainy, none of them ever thought of providing for his own security by disclosing the fraud ; but that amidst sufferings the most grievous to flesh and blood, they persevered in their conspiracy to cheat the world into piety, honesty, and benevolence." " Truly," adds the Principal, "they who can swallow such suppositions, have no title to object to miracles."*

In opposition to all this, however, it is alleged by the assailants of the miracles, that the statements of the witnesses do not harmonize, but that, in their different accounts, there are so many discrepancies

---

* Lectures in Divinity, by George Hill, D.D. Vol. I., pp. 47, 48.

TESTIMONY IN BEHALF OF MIRACLES. 127

and contradictions as to destroy entirely the value of their testimony. Thoroughly to answer this objection would require us to take up and examine every case of alleged inconsistency and show either that it is possible that the accounts may be all correct, despite their apparent antagonism, or that even if it be impossible for us, with our limited knowledge of the original circumstances, to explain how they are all in harmony, still there is nothing in the existence of such things to warrant our disbelief of the testimony of the evangelists where they thoroughly agree. To do that, however, would need a bulky volume for itself, since it is well known that an objection may be stated in a line which it would require a dissertation to remove. I content myself, therefore, with referring to the explanations given in our best commentaries of the alleged discrepancies, and I offer merely a few general considerations on the whole subject, without seeking to enter into detail.

It is to be remembered, then, that a certain degree of diversity is to be expected in four depositions—which profess to be, and which really are—separate and independent of each other. If you enter into a court of law, and take note of the testimony given by different individuals to the same facts, you will not fail to remark that there are characteristic traits in every deposition. Each witness describes what he saw from his own angle of observation, and in minor details each one expresses himself differently from another; but to the great facts, they all, if truthful, bear the most distinct and unequivocal testimony. Now, as the evangelists are witnesses of matters of fact, or at least give the statements of those who were witnesses, we may expect similar diversity in their narratives if they be independent and distinct. Had they all agreed in every minute phasis of description, their value as distinct witnesses would have been destroyed; and it might have been said, that, though they were four in name, they were in reality but one —each repeating like an echo what the other had said. There are here two possibilities—either four narratives alike in everything, and so bearing the marks of collusion and arrangement, or four accounts as we really have them, with distinctive differences and indications of independence of each other, yet agreeing in the same great and important particulars. Now every one who knows anything of the laws of evidence will declare that witnesses of the latter character are immensely more valuable, and reliable than of the former. Hence, the discrepancies of which so much is made by antagonists are really unavoidable, if we would have the best and least suspicious kind of testimony. It is here, as we have seen it on former occasions—the man who is disposed to find fault will make a fault however it may be. Give him accounts *verbatim et literatim* the same, and *that* will be evidence of designed imposture; give him accounts differing apparently in some minor respects from each other, while yet agreeing substantially, and *that* is made a reason why they should not be believed; but the man of common sense will at once see and admit that minor discrepancy is always to be expected when we have different and independent witnesses.

Again, it must not be forgotten that the depositions here are in writing, and that we cannot do with a document precisely as we would with a witness whom we are examining *viva voce*. There is no doubt a sort of cross-examination made by every good interpreter of Scripture when he submits each separate statement to a rigid analysis and endeavors to see precisely what it means; but even that, valuable as it has been in removing the appearance of discrepancy on many occasions, is not for a moment to be compared with the advantage for the elucidation of truth which is furnished by oral examination in the witness box.

While I lived in Liverpool, I frequently embraced the opportunity afforded me in an assize town of spending a few hours in a court of justice, and have seen with no little admiration, how, under the guidance of the judge and by the acuteness of the counsel on both sides, the whole truth has been gradually evolved. Repeatedly have I heard one witness seem to contradict another far more thoroughly than any one of the evangelists appears to contravene another; and yet a question has been put by the bar, or the bench, or the jury, the answer to which has brought out some new fact by which harmony has been restored—or, perhaps the former witness has been recalled, and a question put to him which has elicited particulars of which before he had said nothing, and the knowledge of which was all that was needed to explain the difference that had appeared. Now this source of information we cannot have in dealing with the Gospels. Here the record is closed; no new fact can be evolved by cross-examination; and so we are deprived of a great means of throwing light upon the matters in dispute. This is a very important consideration, especially when we take into account the fact that the great mass of discrepancies which have been heaped together by the labors of objectors consists of such as arise out of our unacquaintance with the whole circumstances; and the answers to a question or two, like those to which we have referred, would go very far to settle the whole matter in each case. One, whose labors in this field give him a right to speak with some weight, has said that "if we knew the real process of the transactions themselves, that knowledge would enable us to give an account of the diversities of narration and arrangement which the Gospels now present to us."*

---

* Alford's Greek Testament, Vol. I., Prolegomena, p. 28.

Two winters ago, as I was returning on a Sunday evening from my church to my home, I was told that a great fire was raging in the city. When I made enquiry into its character, I was told by a member of my family that the first account which she received from a passer-by was that it was a chair-factory; the second, from another casual informant, was, that it was an armory; and the third, from still another source, was, that it was a church; and she did not know which to believe. According to the logic of those who assail the Gospel discrepancies, she ought to have come to the conclusion that there was no fire at all. But on the following morning, when I opened my newspaper, I found that all three reports were true, and that even if there had been a fourth—to the effect that two churches had been destroyed—that also would have been correct. Now, a case like that occurring at one's own door-step, may well guard us against hastily assuming that an apparent discrepancy is necessarily an entire contradiction; for, though there is a difference between an accidental fire and a miracle, the logic of evidence is the same in both, and where the testimony to the main matter is clear, and given by persons in other respects trustworthy, and with no conceivable motive impelling them to deceive, we are warranted in concluding that if we knew all the facts, every minor discrepancy would disappear.

Now we must not lose sight of the truth, that with all their appearance of diversity in some details, the Gospel writers yet concur in bearing testimony to the great fact that Jesus wrought miracles. About the surroundings of some of them they may seem to vary one from another, but as to the fact that He wrought the miracles they agree; and in these circumstances any unbiased mind seeking to give an impartial verdict would at once accept their statement as to the matters in which they are at one, reserving his judgment as to those in regard to which they seem to differ. Let it be observed that I am arguing here, not as to the nature or extent of the inspiration claimed for these narratives—that is an after-question; at present I am concerned only with their credibility; and though it would not, I think, be difficult to answer all the objections which might be brought against the plenary theory of inspiration from these apparent inconsistencies, yet I may not encumber myself now with such considerations. I am dealing simply with their credibility; and the position which I here take up is, that since we have found that the witnesses agree in certain great and important matters, among which is the fact that Jesus performed miracles, and since we have seen that the men themselves are both morally and intellectually trustworthy, therefore we may fairly hold as proved the things in which they are in perfect harmony, without waiting to determine what is the precise truth as to those things in which they appear to be at variance. I do not say, observe, that in regard to these last it is in every case impossible precisely to discover what was the true order of occurrences (for in many instances a patient study of the records has led to a solution of the difficulty, though there are others of which all explanation must be mainly conjectured); yet even if this were impossible, we must not allow ourselves on that account to reject the things in which *such* witnesses agree; and in laying down this principle, I feel I would be supported by the authority of every judge on the bench. There is scarcely a trial of importance on record in which there has not been some particular concerning which there has been difficulty, uncertainty, and discrepancy, and about which it has been felt to be almost impossible to get at the precise truth. Almost every *cause célèbre* has had its mystery, which, in spite of the facilities afforded by cross-examination, has not been thoroughly cleared up; nevertheless, that has not prevented the jury from coming to a verdict on those things in the evidence which were clear. Now, I ask that the testimony of the evangelists shall be treated in the same way, and then I am sure that every intelligent enquirer will give his voice in favor of the reality and genuineness of the miracles of Christ. No more striking illustration of the principle on which I am now insisting can be found than that which is furnished by the case of our Lord's resurrection, and in presenting it to you I gladly avail myself of the words of Dean Alford: "What can be more undoubted and unanimous than the testimony of the evangelists to THE RESURRECTION OF THE LORD? If there be one fact rather than another of which the apostles were witnesses, *it was this;* and in the concurrent narratives of all four evangelists it stands related beyond all cavil or question. Yet of all the events which they have described, *none is so variously put forth in detail*, or with so many minor discrepancies. And this was just what might have been expected on the principles above laid down. The great fact that the Lord *was risen*—set forth by the ocular witness of the apostles who had seen Him—became from that day first in importance in the delivery of their testimony. "The *precise order* of His appearances would naturally, from the overwhelming nature of their present emotions, be a matter of minor consequence, and perhaps not even of accurate enquiry till some time had passed. Then, with the utmost desire on the part of the women and apostles to collect the events in the exact order of time, some confusion would be apparent in the history, and some discrepancies in versions of it, which were the results of separate and independent enquiries, the traces of which pervade our present accounts. But what fair-judging student of the Gospels ever made these variations or discrepancies a ground for doubting the veracity of the evangelists as to the fact of the resurrection, or the principal details of our Lord's appearance after it?"*

We may not quite agree with the Dean's conjectural theory as to the origination of the variations, but no one who has given attention to the laws of evidence will cavil with the principle on which he proceeds; and we are convinced that if the few real discrepancies (if, indeed, they be real), were looked at in the light in which we have here put them, they would not be felt as any difficulty in the way of the reception of the testimony of the apostles to the miraculous occurrences in the history of our Lord, where it is consentaneous and clear.

---
* Alford's Greek Testament, Vol. I., Prolegomena, pp. 19, 20.

THE MYTHICAL THEORY.

LECTURE V.

THE MYTHICAL THEORY.

2 Peter i. 16: We have not followed cunningly-devised fables.

IN opposition to the weighty evidence, of which I attempted to give a summary, in my last lecture, the most recent antagonists of the supernatural have attempted to show that the stories of the miracles of Christ, contained in the four gospels, originated in such a way as to be perfectly consistent with probability, while yet they do not describe actual occurrences. They have, in fact, applied the theory of development to the formation of the evangelic narratives, and have tried to show how round a very small nucleus of fact, a great mass of legends have grouped themselves in a way that is, in their estimation, at least, not only natural, but probable.

The great pioneer in this department was Dr. D. F. Strauss, in his " Life of Jesus Critically Considered." He has been followed in France, though with certain not unimportant modifications, by Ernest Renan; and in Holland, by Kuenen, Oort, and Hooykaas, in that work which, under an English dress, has recently acquired a newspaper notoriety among us. It will be impossible, within the compass of a single lecture, to track these writers through all the mazes of their ingenious subtlety; yet my treatment of the subject of miracles would be lacking in completeness, if I did not examine, with some degree of thoroughness, the theory on which, with specific differences among themselves, they all profess to work.

A myth, according to Strauss, is a religious idea clothed in a historic form. That form may either be a pure fiction, or it may have a nucleus of fact, enlarged and modified or embellished by the ideas which have sought through it to find expression. He distinguishes between myths and legends. A myth is "an idea translated by mental realism into fact; a legend is a group of ideas round a nucleus of fact;" and he endeavors to show that if a small basis of fact heightened by legend be allowed in the Gospel history, the influence of myth will account for the remainder. To borrow from the Critical Historian of Free Thought, "the idea is regarded as prior to the fact; the need of a deliverer, he pretends, created the idea of a Saviour; the misinterpretation of old prophecy presented conditions which, in the popular mind, must be fulfilled by the Messiah. The Gospel history is regarded as the attempt of the idea to realize itself in fact."* Thus viewed, the facts of the his-

---

* A. S. Farrar's "Critical History of Free Thought," p. 380.

THE MYTHICAL THEORY. 141

tory of Jesus are reduced to the fewest possible number. He was brought up at Nazareth; He was baptized by John; He formed disciples, whom He impressed with His wisdom and goodness; He taught in the various districts of Palestine; He proclaimed the Messianic kingdom; He opposed the outwardness of the Pharisees; and provoked their enmity, so that they put Him to death upon the cross;—such is the substance of our Lord's history, which remains after the gospels have been subjected to the criticism of Strauss, and round these facts the ideas and aspirations of the early Christians wove the stories which we find now under the names of the Evangelists, imagination lending itself not only to glorify, but also, in a great degree, to create the object of faith. These books are thus regarded, not as the records of actual occurrences, but as the embodiment of the ideas which the Jews entertained of their Messiah; and much of their coloring is attributed to the Old Testament Scriptures, with which the people had been so long familiar. Thus the visit of the wise men to Bethlehem is viewed as suggested by the prophecy of Balaam; the massacre of the infants by Herod is held to correspond to the destruction of the Hebrew children by Pharaoh; the flight into Egypt is regarded as having sprung out of the flight of Moses into Midian; the appearance of Jesus in the temple at the age of twelve is said to have been derived from similar records regarding Samuel; the temptation is considered as an embodiment of the idea brought out in the history of Job, that good men are the objects of special hatred to Satan; and the transfiguration is thought to be accounted for by describing it as an adaptation to Jesus of the narrative of the glory which shone on Moses' face at Sinai. These are specimens of the method pursued by Strauss and his followers, his first theory being that all this was done, not by any one individual, or with any fraudulent design, but that it was what one has called "a gradual and spontaneous aggregation about the person of Jesus of the various types and analogies which the Jews supposed would be realized in the Messiah."* To this source of the narratives there falls to be added the legendary portion derived from the influence of Jesus; and these together, he contends, serve to account for the documents as they are now in our possession. Such is the mythical theory, in its original form, but there are many objections to it, each of which is fatal.

It is admitted, of course, that in the cases of Greece and Rome, as also in that of India, there are religious myths, which must be regarded as unhistorical; but we contend that there are certain marked differences between these and the records of the miracles of Christ, which forbid us to place them both in the same cate-

---

* "British and Foreign Evangelical Review," Vol. I., pp. 630, 631.

gory. In particular, we find a perfect harmony between the characteristics of Jesus as a worker of miracles, and those which come out in the other chapters of His history, which is not perceived between the ordinary actions of other mythical heroes, and their bearing in the doing of the wonders which have grouped themselves around their names. The miracles of our Lord, taken in connection with the circumstances and the manner in which they were performed, tell us as much of His disposition, as do His ordinary conversations, and what we may call His common works, and He is the same Jesus in them both. Nay, it may even be affirmed, that notwithstanding their repudiation of the supernatural, much of that impression of His character, which has been received even by those who deny His deity, has been unconsciously derived by them from their perusal of the history of His supernatural works. How little, for example, we should know of His tenderness, His sympathy, His compassion, His humility, His wisdom, His discrimination between the various classes of those with whom He came into contact, if all the stories of His miracles were to be eliminated from the gospels. And yet, all of these traits, as they thus reveal themselves before our eyes, in connection with His miracles, are not only perfectly consistent, but also beautifully in harmony with His character, as it comes out in His conversations and conduct at other times. Any one can see at a glance that He who wept at the grave of Lazarus is the same in all the deep sympathy of His nature, as He who spoke the last consolatory address to His disciples; and there is the same homogeneity between His bearing in His other miracles and the substance of His discourses. Now this feature is conspicuously absent in the mythical stories of other religions. They are not only in many instances ridiculous in their extravagance, but also generally associated with manifestations of temper, which degrade the hero, in the very moment when the greatness of his power is glorified, while sometimes they indicate a disposition which is in direct contradiction to that which comes out in him elsewhere. This argument has been admirably elaborated by a recent writer from whom I quote the following sentences: "The tenderest of all the Greeks, 'Euripides, the human,' drew no fairer picture than the restoration by Herakles of the wife of Admetos from the grave. Yet the demi-god spices for himself, with a little cruelty, the tamer bliss of his beneficence, forcing Alkestis, unrecognized, and almost, as they complain, by violence, into the house of mourning, telling her bereaved husband that the longing for a new bridal will relieve his woe, and playing so roughly with the wound he means to heal, that at the last the cry is wrenched from the sufferer: 'Silence; what have you said? I would not have believed it of you.'"* When we contrast this with the bearing of Jesus at the resurrection of Lazarus, we see a distinct difference between the two in the manner of the miracle-worker, while at the same we mark in the demeanor of Jesus, "the same beautiful union of quick sympathy, with sharp intelligence resulting in perfect tact," which we observe, also, to be characteristic of Him in those portions of the gospels which even the most negative critics are willing to accept as genuine. Max Müller, quoted by the same author, has said: "The Buddhist legends teem with miserable miracles attributed to Buddha and his disciples, miracles which, for wonders, certainly surpass the miracles of any other religion. Yet, in their own sacred Canon, a saying of Buddha is recorded, prohibiting his disciples from working miracles."†

But, indeed, we need go no farther here than the apocryphal gospels, to be convinced of the difference between the writings of the four evangelists and all mythical productions. We feel at once on reading these that the Jesus whom they depict is not the Jesus whom the sacred writers have delineated. These books are clearly mythical, and the difference between them and the canonical Scriptures—not only

---

* "Christ Bearing Witness to Himself," by Rev. G. A. Chadwick, D.D., p. 23.
† Ibid., p. 137.

in style, but in the portraiture which they give of Jesus—is both striking and suggestive. The Gospel of the Infancy depicts a boy who became the terror of the neighborhood, and whose temper was always flashing out in some miracle of punishment, but the homogeneousness in the character of Jesus as He appears in these four histories, whether as a miracle-worker or as a simple teacher, is so remarkable that it cannot be accounted for on the principle that they were what we may call a "fortuitous combination" of marvellous stories. It might have been the work of design, though it would have required the genius of a Shakespeare and more to produce it, and there was no such genius among the apostles. But it certainly never could have resulted from spontaneous aggregation, and the simplest explanation of their origin, one, too, which, save for their pre-determination to admit no miracles, would have commended itself to all critics, is that given by the writers themselves, namely, that they were testifying what they themselves had seen and heard.

Again, it is not to be forgotten that myths belong to the childhood of history. Every one knows that the mythologies of Greece and Rome were generated in the pre-historic ages. But that in which the Gospels were produced was pre-eminently not merely a historic, but a sceptical age. The Greeks and Romans were beginning to question their own religious stories, and it is hardly credible that in such an era a new mythology should arise.

Moreover, myths require time for their growth, and, therefore, this theory is utterly inconsistent with the date at which our gospels were written. So sensible was Strauss of the force of this objection, that he has attempted to fix the time at which these were completed at about the middle of the second century. But, in this respect, he is at variance with the great majority of critics, and even with some of the school to which he himself belonged. The full elucidation of this matter belongs to another branch of the Christian evidences. But Mr. Sanday, in his recent elaborate monograph on the fourth gospel, has made it plain to every candid reader that the narrative of John was written by an eye-witness, and must, therefore, belong to the first century;* and, as it is universally conceded that it was the latest of the four, the others must be placed somewhere in the third quarter of the first century; that is to say, they were finished between the years 50 and 75 of the Christian era. We have thus only thirty years or a little more allowed for the spontaneous aggregation of those so-called fictions around the small nucleus of

---

* The same conclusion is reached in the full, candid, and exhaustive introduction to his commentary on John by Canon Westcott in the "Speaker's Commentary," and by Dr. Ezra Abbot in his recent monograph on the same subject which appeared in the *Unitarian Review*.

facts which they are admitted to contain. Their date is as near to the events which they describe as this year is to 1848; and so it would be as easy for us to fabricate a mass of myths round the revolutions of that year in Europe, and the subsequent *coup d'etât* by which Louis Napoleon took possession of the throne of France, as it was for the Evangelists to weave a tissue of marvels round the name of Jesus.

But we are not left here to deal with the gospels alone. The most sceptical critics have been compelled to admit the genuineness of at least four of Paul's epistles—those to the Galatians, Corinthians, and Romans—and in these we have statements which indicate that at the time at which they were written, the great facts which the gospels narrate concerning Jesus were known and believed. Now these letters must all be put between the years 50 and 60 of our era, and so Paul was writing not much more than twenty years after the crucifixion. Yet, in them we have repeated reference to the death and resurrection of Christ. One of them gives us an account of the institution of the Lord's Supper, another of them uses language which suggests the Deity of the person of Christ, and all of them pre-suppose in their readers such a knowledge of the facts of the history of Jesus, that, though they were written before the gospels, we feel that in our New Testament they are fitly placed after them, inasmuch as they can be properly understood only by those who are familiar with the incidents which the gospels narrate.

Now, how could such myths as these spring up and be generally received and believed among Christians within the space of twenty years? We might as well expect that supernatural marvels should by this time have clustered round the name of George Groves, the friend and some time patron of John Kitto, and one of the earliest of the Plymouth Brethren; or that of Alexander Campbell, who originated the sect of Baptists, which is commonly called after him.

Besides, taking the gospels as we find them, the last of the four is that which has the fewest records of miracles in it. If, therefore, there had been any tendency among the genuine followers of Jesus at that early date toward the aggregation of such stories round the name of Jesus, it is inconceivable that the latest gospel, which was farthest removed from the year of the crucifixion, should have the smallest number of such things in it; and the farther down the stream of time you put that gospel, the more inconceivable does this become.

But more, and even more important than anything which I have yet advanced, the theory of Strauss fails to account in any satisfactory manner—both for the origin of the character of Jesus as presented in the gospels, and for the origin of the Church itself.

He tells us, indeed, that the myths were already to a large extent made to hand in the Old Testament, and that the Jews only transferred their ideas of the Messiah to Jesus. But to this the reply is easy; for the notion of the Messiah then prevalent, and indeed too long clung to even by the first disciples of Jesus, was very different from—was in many respects precisely the opposite of, that which was realized in Jesus; so that it is palpably absurd to suppose that they clothed His history with the dress of their own imagination. Besides, the Jesus of the gospels was rejected by the Jews, and His followers latterly were mainly from among the Gentiles. By the time the gospels were written the Gentiles formed a large proportion of the Church; and who that thinks of the circumcision controversy and the division which it created, can suppose that the non-Jewish portion of the community would be content to receive the ready-made ideas of the Jews as to their Messiah? Taking into consideration, therefore, the Gentile elements in the Church, the attempt to trace the Gospel narratives to mere Jewish idealism must be pronounced a failure.

But further, how on such a theory are we to account for the origin of the Church itself? In the view of Strauss, the Christ of the gospels is the creation of the Church. But whence came the Church itself? How did it originate? The ordinary inquirer traces its origin to the life, death, and resurrection of Jesus. And in this view all is plain; for such a cause is adequate to the production of the effect. The terms of salvation according to Paul were these: "If thou shalt confess with thy mouth the Lord Jesus, and shalt believe in thine heart that God hath raised him from the dead, thou shalt be saved."* The Church stood upon this foundation; but if the resurrection is a myth, who or what supported the Church till that myth was created? Admit that the resurrection is a fact, and then all is explained; but deny that, and how shall we account for the existence of the Church which stood upon it? Men do not begin to build a house at the roof. The pedestal must be reared before the statue can be put upon it. The Church could not be formed without the belief in the resurrection of Christ. How, then, could the Church have created the myth which tells of that resurrection? This is very strongly put by Mr. Row in the following paragraph:

"It is evident that some event must have taken place within a few days after the crucifixion, which has been capable of supporting the whole weight of the Christian Church. The actual resurrection of Jesus would have been a sufficient historical basis on which it could have been erected. This the believers

---

* Rom. x. 9.

in the mythic theory pronounce to be impossible to have happened as a fact. It was necessary, therefore, that it should have been invented as a fiction, and that the followers of Jesus should have been induced to believe in it as a fact. Such an invention would have been much easier after the lapse of years. A considerable interval of time would have afforded the opportunity for the impression of the crucifixion to have grown faint. But if our opponents concede a period of years for the elaboration of this fiction, they will greatly exhaust the time at their command for the creation of the conception of Christ. In addition to this, while the belief is being created, the Church is perishing."*

These considerations, therefore, are enough to prove both that this theory is improbable in itself, and fails to account for the facts of the case. Its author deals with the evangelic narratives in a manner which is continually landing him in inconsistencies and contradictions. He denies the authenticity of the gospels, and yet when it serves his purpose to do so, he refers to them as if they were of the most credible character. He takes what suits him, and then ignores the rest, or dismisses it as mythical. At one time he regards them as the result of a very simple process going on almost imperceptibly and with-

---

* "The Jesus of the Gospels," by Rev. C. A. Row, pp. 262, 263.

out any fraudulent intention in the minds of thousands at once; at another, when perhaps he is dealing with some details, he assumes a degree of study and reflection on the part of their originators, which is absolutely incompatible with the absence of design. His method, if rigidly applied to other records, would make all history impossible. He starts with a foregone conclusion. Everything consistent, or which, with a little manipulation, can be made consistent with that, he retains; and all else, on one pretence or another, he rejects. He is not sparing of dogmatism; and has at command a whole corps of reserve resources to which in times of perplexity he betakes himself. He sets forth in imposing array the list of discrepancies, real or imaginary, between the evangelists, and that, too, in the most glaring form, apparently altogether oblivious of the explanations which many of them have received; and he works wonders by the mere "silence" of Josephus. But who does not see that, by a similar process, any history may be rendered mythical? Just as Whately's "Historic Doubts" as to the existence of Napoleon Buonaparte exposed the falsehood of Hume's principles, so others have applied the principles of Strauss to certain well-known chapters of modern history, and have, by a *reductio ad absurdum*, shown the hollowness of the mythical theory. And, indeed, in his latest work on the "Life of Christ," Strauss virtually abandoned it himself, for in it, to use his own words, he "allowed more room than before to the hypothesis of conscious and intentional fiction;" and so ultimately he took his place among those who reckon the authors of the gospels as deliberate deceivers, thereby laying himself open to the full force of the argument which shows the absurdity of the idea that the purest morality the world has ever seen, has been developed out of a lie. But as others have taken up that which he ultimately discarded, the examination to which I have subjected his theory cannot be regarded as unnecessary, and has prepared us for entering with more intelligence on the analysis of that of Renan.

The French author differs from his German forerunner in preferring the legendary to the mythical in the source of the gospels, because, "while giving large scope for the operation of popular opinion, it allows the action and personal influence of Jesus to remain entire." Let me give you an idea of his theory, as far as possible, in his own words: "The legends about Jesus were the fruit of a great and entirely spontaneous conspiracy, and were developed around him during his life-time."* " The title, Son of David, was the first which he accepted, probably without being concerned in the innocent frauds by which it

---

* Renan's " Life of Jesus," as before, pp. 179, 180.

was sought to secure it unto Him. . . . . He allowed a title to be given him, without which he could not hope for success. He ended, it seems, by taking pleasure therein; for he performed most willingly the miracles (*i. e.*, in Renan's, view the feats or tricks which passed for miracles), which were asked of him by those who used this title in addressing him."* "As to miracles, they were regarded at this period as an indispensable mark of the divine and as the sign of the prophetic vocation. . . . . Jesus was, therefore, obliged to choose between two alternatives: either to renounce his mission or to become a miracle-worker."† "It is probable that the hearers of Jesus were more struck by his miracles than by his eminently divine discourses. Let us add that, doubtless, popular rumor, both before and after the death of Jesus, exaggerated enormously the number of occurrences of this kind."‡ "We will admit without hesitation that acts which would now be considered as acts of illusion or folly, held a large place in the life of Jesus."§ "We must remember that every idea loses something of its purity as soon as it aspires to realize itself. Success is never attained without some injury being done to the sensibility of the soul. Such is the feebleness of the human mind, that the best causes are ofttimes gained by the worst arguments."‖

---

* Ibid., p. 178.   † Ibid., p. 189.   ‡ Ibid., p. 190.
§ Ibid., p. 190.   ‖ Ibid., p. 190.

"Nothing great has been established that does not rest upon a legend. The only culprit in such cases is the humanity which is willing to be deceived."* "History is impossible, if we do not fully admit that there are many standards of sincerity. All great things are done through the people; now we can only lead the people by adapting ourselves to its ideas. The philosopher who, knowing this, isolates and fortifies himself in his integrity, is highly praiseworthy; but he who takes humanity with its illusions, and seeks to act with it and upon it, cannot be blamed. It is easy for us, who are so powerless, to call this falsehood; when we have effected by our scruples what they accomplished by their falsehood, we shall have a right to be severe upon them."†

The very citation of these extracts is enough to condemn this theory, not only because of the Jesuitical morality which they advocate, but also because as we see from them they seek to evolve truth out of falsehood, and sincerity out of deceit. The legendary hypothesis in this form brings back upon us all the moral anomalies, or, to call them by their right name, impossibilities, which are inseparable from the very conception of deception in such an one as Jesus was, whether we consider His character as portrayed in the gospels, or the effects which His life and work have

---

* Renan's "Life of Jesus," as before, p. 195.   † Ibid., p. 187.

produced on humanity; and substitutes for a perfectly adequate explanation of these effects, one which is both unnatural, unphilosophical, and improbable.

Three things, I desire to set pointedly before you concerning this attempt to construct a modern romance out of the Gospel narratives, while eliminating from them every element of the supernatural.

In the first place, it is inconsistent with itself. When we ask how Jesus came to be called the Son of David, Renan gives us for answer, that He "allowed a title to be given him without which he could not look for success," and when we enquire how He came to have miracles associated with Him, the reply is that "he professed to work them, because without that he could not have been received as the Messiah, one of whose well-known appellations was the Son of David." Now, let us analyze these statements. When were these miracles wrought by Jesus? They must have been performed either before or after He was received as the Messiah. If before, then it could not be said that He merely allowed Himself to be called by a name, to obtain which was the very purpose for which the miracles—as Renan understands miracles —were wrought by Him; if after, then He did not need to work them in order to be received as the Messiah, for He was already so recognized. If Jesus had the title in a manner forced upon Him, He could not have wrought miracles with the view of getting it; if He wrought miracles for the purpose of being received as the Messiah, then when He was so received, He cannot be said merely to have allowed Himself to be so called. The questions recur, How did the belief that He was the Messiah originate? and, How came He to attract to Himself the abiding allegiance of those who formed the first members of His Church?—and to these questions Renan gives no answer any more than Strauss.

But, in the second place, this theory of Renan is held by him in connection with a view of the origin of the written gospels, which on the very face of it is inconsistent with possibility. He yields so far to the force of evidence as to admit that all the four were completed before the end of the first century.* He dates that of Luke only a short time before the destruction of Jerusalem, and would, so far as appears, have put it earlier than that, save for the reason that it contains a prediction of that event, and, of course, that could not have been written before the event occurred, for that would be a miracle, and miracles in his view are impossible. He regards the

---

* Renan's "Life of Jesus," as before, p. 1. But it needs to be added that after considerable wavering and vacillation he has, in his most recent utterances on the subject, accepted A.D. 125 as the date of the gospel by John. This, however, for the reason suggested on a previous page, only increases the difficulty, for it leaves unaccounted for the fact that the fourth gospel has the record of fewer miracles than the others.

THE MYTHICAL THEORY. 159

third gospel as having been produced at a later date than the first two. Now, with these admissions in mind, listen to his account of the Genesis and Exodus of the first two gospels. They are "impersonal compositions in which the author totally disappears. That which appears most likely is that we have not the entirely original compilations of either Matthew or Mark, but that our first two gospels are versions in which the attempt is made to fill up the gaps of the one text by the other. Every one wished, in fact, to possess a complete copy. He who had in his copy only discourses, wished to have narratives, and *vice versa*. It is thus that the gospel according to Matthew is found to have included almost all the anecdotes of Mark, and that the gospel according to Mark now contains numerous features which came from the *logia* of Matthew."* " There was no scruple in inserting additions, in variously combining them, and in completing some by others. The poor man who has but one book wishes that it may contain all that is dear to his heart. These little books were lent : each one transcribed in the margin of his copy the words and the parables he found elsewhere, which touched him. The most beautiful thing in the world has thus proceeded from an obscure and purely popular elaboration." † Now, over and above the fact that

---

* Renan's " Life of Jesus," as before, pp. 10, 11.
† Ibid., p. 12.

he offers not the shadow of a shade of proof of these assertions, let us see how improbable they are in themselves. Remember, that on his own showing, these two gospels appeared before that of Luke, which is in his view "a much more advanced compilation."* Remember, also, that the gospel of Luke, again on his own admission, was written shortly after the destruction of Jerusalem, which occurred in A.D. 70. We must, therefore, even on his own ground, place the gospels of Matthew and Mark in the decade between 60 and 70 A.D., so that for the purely popular elaboration of which he has spoken, we have only an allowance of thirty years, which, considering the rarity of manuscripts and the difficulty of producing them in those days, is utterly inadequate for the purpose.

But how ludicrously impossible is this account of these two gospels! Renan forgets that he has to do with documents which were not simply private possessions, but the public property of the churches. However possible, therefore, it might be for the poor man with his one book to have added on the margin of his own copy the accounts of incidents, or the reports of discourses, which interested him, the thing to be explained is the public reception of these two separate books in their present form by the churches;

---

* Renan's "Life of Jesus," as before, p. 9.

and we boldly say, that his attempt to do that is absurd. Suppose that such a process as he has imagined had been really carried on, then what must have been the issue? Clearly either one great aggregate agglomeration of the two gospels, in which what was Matthew's and what was Mark's would be indistinguishable, or an endless number of separate compilations, each formed according to the taste of him that made it, and consisting of the portions which "touched him" most tenderly. But, instead, we have two books bearing very clear marks of separate individuality. It would take more time than I have now at command to bring out the traces of the author's idiosyncrasies in the gospel by Matthew,* but it may be worth while to give a brief summary of the peculiarities of Mark—the rather, as it is too generally taken for granted that the recorded gospel is but an epitome of the first.

Absolutely shorter than that of Matthew, it will yet be found that the narrative of Mark is in many instances more full, detailed, and explicit than that of his brother evangelist; and every one who has given himself to the study of Gospel Harmony knows, that very frequently the element that is needed to explain the apparent discrepancy between the others is supplied by Mark. In particular, his gospel is dis-

---

* See Appendix, Note C.

tinguished by the graphic portraiture of events in the present tense. He places the whole circumstances before his readers' eyes, and with his often recurring "straightway,"* he gives a vivid distinctness to each occurrence. Then we find that more attention is bestowed by him on the works of Jesus than on His words, so that we have comparatively few of the Lord's discourses preserved in his chapters. This circumstance is fatal to the theory we are considering; for if those who had a record of the works wished one of the discourses, and *vice versa*, then how comes it that so few discourses are in Mark? As one has very well remarked here: "Mark is silent on the greatest of these discourses which Matthew records. What were the persons about who wished to have a complete copy out of the two, and yet forgot to adopt the Sermon on the Mount? Two very small books, subjected to this process of active assimilation, still show marks of independence in every chapter, and the background of resemblances throws out the differences into stronger relief. Had the object been to produce one gospel out of two, any unskilful hand, used freely for a couple of days, would have produced a more successful result than a whole community, working as M. Renan supposes,

---

* Εὐθέως, ἐυθὺς. These two terms taken together occur no fewer than forty-one times in the second gospel.

has done."* But more minute individualisms even than those which we have noted appear in Mark; for to him it is that we are mainly indebted for the information we have regarding our Lord's looks, gestures, and feelings. It is he who tells us that " He looked round upon His accusers with anger, being grieved for the hardness of their hearts."† To him we owe the statement that He was " much displeased" with the disciples for commanding away the children from Him.‡ He speaks of His look of love directed to His spiritual children ; § His look of reproof on the disciples as a whole, and specially on Peter ;‖ His beholding in love the young man who came to Him ;¶ and His looking round about upon His disciples in the enforcement of His words.** So, too, regarding the incidents in the career of Peter, with whom Mark is generally connected, a similar individuality appears, bringing out a modesty of nature which we do not commonly associate with that apostle, but in which we recognize how much the grace of God had subdued the inherent forwardness of the man. There is the absence of reference to the honors which Christ bestowed upon him, and of which the others have spoken. No mention is made of the gift of the keys, or of the walking on the

---

* *North British Review*, No. 79, pp. 189, 190.   † Mark iii. 5.
‡ Mark x. 14.   § Mark iii. 34.   ‖ Chap. viii. 33.
¶ Chap. x. 21.   ** Chap. x. 23–27.

waves, or of the feet-washing, or of the scene by the Sea of Galilee; while, on the other hand, the reproof given him by the Lord immediately after his promise about the keys is inserted, and we have furnished to us a full and particular account of the details of his denial of his Master.

Only in one instance does there seem to be a departure from this rule, which the author appears to have studiously followed, and that is when, after Christ's resurrection, the command is given: " Go, tell His disciples and Peter;"* but even this is no exception, for it is there as a mark of the Divine condescension and generous love of Jesus to him even after his thrice-repeated sin, and is inserted not to do honor to Peter, but to give glory to his Lord.

On the whole, then, we may allege that the distinctive characteristics of this gospel are too strongly marked to admit of our reception of any such theory in regard to its origin as that which Renan has propounded; and we may leave the matter to the judgment of the unbiased mind, merely quoting the remarks of a recent commentator in regard to this very precious, but we fear too greatly neglected book:

" What strikes every one is, that though the briefest of all the gospels, this is, in some of the principal scenes of our Lord's history, the fullest. But what

---

* Mark xvi. 7.

THE MYTHICAL THEORY. 165

is not so obvious is, that wherever the finer and subtler feelings of humanity, or the deeper and more peculiar hues of our Lord's character were brought out, these, though they should be lightly passed over by all the other evangelists, are sure to be found here, and in touches of such quiet delicacy and power, that, though scarcely observed by the cursory reader, they leave indelible impressions upon all the thoughtful, and furnish a key to much that is in the other gospels."*

Renan is not more successful in his treatment of the gospel of John, but this must suffice as a specimen of the improbabilities and inconsistencies in which he is landed by his attempt to account, on his principles, for the formation of these narratives, whose simple naturalness has charmed every reader, in spite of his prepossessions and prejudices against them.

But, to bring our analysis and argument to a close, we emphasize, in the third place, the fact that the theory of Renan involves all the moral incongruities which we have seen are inseparable from the opinion that Jesus was, in any sense of the word, a deceiver. For a deceiver He was, if this is the true account, and all the miracles are degraded to mere acts of illusion, performed for the purpose of substantiating a claim to which He had no shadow of a title. Renan, indeed,

---

* Dr. David Brown in "Commentary: Critical, Experimental, and Practical," Vol. V., under Mark I.

attempts to vindicate Him for His imposture by a species of casuistry; but his vindication is a failure. True, he says that "a mere sorcerer after the manner of Simon, the magician, could not have brought about a moral revolution like that effected by Jesus,"* but the question here is, Could the author of a moral revolution like that effected by Jesus, employ such immoral means as that of palming Himself upon the people as a worker of real miracles, while He was only a thaumaturgus, that is, a performer of acts of illusion and folly? Thus are we brought back to the point which we reached in our former argument: either Jesus was a deceiver and knowingly passed off as miracles what were only feats of legerdemain—and so we are beset with all the moral difficulties on which we have enlarged—or He was the truth, and His miracles were genuine. To the character of Jesus himself, and the influence of the system which He introduced, this, like all our other modern religious controversies, narrows in; and we do not shrink from the issue;—for if that pure and holy character be sullied, the miracles are not worth the keeping; while if that be retained spotless, the miracles will present no difficulty, since the character of Jesus is itself the grandest miracle the world has ever seen. Not from a root of deception could such a goodly tree, bearing on its branches

---

* Renan, as before, p. 95.

all manner of wholesome fruits, and whose leaves are for the healing of the nations, spring; and we may well say, with an eloquent reviewer, "If falsehood about the holiest things is so blessed with fruit that is not false, then surely there is no such divine rule of truth and justice over the world as we had supposed; and grapes may blossom on thorns and figs be sought among thistles; God blesses alike the truth and the lie; and the record of eighteen centuries of church history is the account of the exuberant vitality of a pious fraud at best, and at most of simple fraud and falsehood. From the edge of this precipice even the non-Christian would try to struggle backward. This moral earthquake where an underlying falsehood shakes all the firm foundations of truth, which we thought solid to the axis, we can only think upon with horror."*

It only remains to be added, that the mythical theory of Strauss has almost disappeared from the place of its birth, and that the good old gospels have reasserted their superiority even in the University of Tubingen. The error thus supplanted in Tubingen has found an asylum for a time in Holland, whence some are seeking to import it into our own land. But we need not fear the issue. Here, as in Germany, it will only bring more investigation to bear upon the

---

* *North British Review*, No. 79, p. 208.

gospels themselves, and the more thoroughly they are examined, the more will the majesty of Jesus reveal itself to the eyes of men, and the more conclusively will it ultimately be shown that no merely natural process can account for the existence of these matchless narratives, and that ineffably glorious personality. One plan after another has been tried to prove that this Christianity of ours is of men, but each new method has been destructive of all the rest, and has been shown to be inconsistent with itself, and not only anti-supernatural, but absolutely unnatural. "They are dead that sought the young child's life." Such was the message that came to Joseph in Egypt, when Herod, who attempted to murder Jesus, had passed away; and such, also, is a summary of the history of the efforts from those of Porphyry and Celus downward, which have been made against the Gospel of the Lord. Out of each new crucible it has come forth with its genuineness more fully tested, and ever, Phœnix-like, it has risen from the fire in which men vainly hoped they had consumed it to ashes. So it has been; so it shall be. Every human key breaks in the lock of the problems which these gospels present; but it opens at once to that which is divine. No mere natural hypothesis will account for the phenomena. But the moment we accept the truth that Jesus is divine, that moment everything in the narratives themselves, and in their influence on our race, is perfectly accounted for. It answers to everything in these as thoroughly as the Copernican theory answers to the phenomena of the solar system. Nothing else so answers to these and explains them, and therefore that must be accepted as the truth.

8

THE EVIDENTIAL VALUE
OF THE
MIRACLES.

LECTURE VI.

THE EVIDENTIAL VALUE OF THE MIRACLES.

Hebrews ii. 4: God also bearing them witness both with signs and wonders and with divers miracles.

THE removal of the objections which have been raised against the possibility and credibility of the Gospel miracles, and the exposure of the unsatisfactory nature of even the most ingenious theories which have been devised for the purpose of accounting on merely natural principles for the origin of the narratives which contain the records of these wondrous works, have brought us now face to face with the question, the miracles being admitted as real— What do they prove? What conclusion are we warranted to draw regarding Jesus from the fact that He wrought supernatural works? Now, if we were right in our definition of a miracle at the outset, this question need not detain us long. We said that a miracle is a work out of the usual sequence of secondary causes and effects, which cannot be accounted for by the ordinary action of these causes, and which is produced by the agency of God, in connection with the word of one who claims to be His representative. Hence, if such works be performed through the instrumentality of, or at the word of, one who claims to be a messenger from God, they are the divine authentication and confirmation of that claim. They are God's attestation of the commission of Him who represents Himself as bearing a communication of His mind to men. They are the credentials of the legate of the Most High, and endorse for us the statements of the ambassador in connection with whose mission they are performed. Their testimony is thus to the doctrine—not immediately and directly, but mediately and through the messenger. Their primary and direct attestation is to him at whose word they are wrought. They represent him as one who is authorized to speak on God's behalf; and thus, through him, they stamp his message as from God.

It has often been said, indeed, that power cannot in the nature of things confirm truth; but that all depends on whose power it is. Now, in this instance it is the power of God, and the moral perfection of Deity gives its own character to the forth-putting of that power in confirmation of the claims of him at whose word the miracle is wrought. The name at the bottom of a letter does not in itself give me a guarantee for the truth of the contents of the epistle; it only tells me who the writer is; and, for my estimate of his statements, I must fall back upon what I know of his character. In like manner, the power of the miracle, taken by itself, does not assure me either of the truthfulness of the claims put forth or the authority of the doctrines taught by the miracle-worker; for that I must fall back on the character of Him whose power performed the supernatural work, and, considering that He is God, I may be well assured that He would not affix the seal of His confirmation to anything that is false, or sanction a claim to speak in His name which is not truthfully advanced.

Thus viewed, miracles are the outward and visible confirmation by supernatural agency of a claim to the possession of an inward commission, equally supernatural, but lying in a region which is beyond the sphere of our observation. The prophet declares that he speaks in God's name the things which God has commanded him; that is to say, he affirms that there is an intellectual and spiritual miracle being wrought upon him, by virtue of which he communicates God's truth to us; but the reality of that mental miracle, so to call it, we have no direct means of testing; and therefore it is attested to us by the performance of another supernatural work—this time in the department of physical nature, and such as we can observe and investigate for ourselves.

When Jesus said to the paralytic, "Son, thy sins

be forgiven thee," He made an assertion, the verification of which was impossible by His hearers; for it referred to that spiritual domain which lies beyond human inspection. Therefore they said, "Why doth this man speak blasphemies? Who can forgive sins but God only?" as if they had exclaimed, "It is a safe thing to make a claim like that, because you know we cannot investigate it." But the Lord, fully aware of their objection, said: "Why reason ye these things in your hearts? Whether is it easier to say to the sick of the palsy, 'Thy sins be forgiven thee,' or to say, 'Arise, take up thy bed and walk?' But that ye may know that the Son of man hath power on earth to forgive sins (he saith to the sick of the palsy) 'I say unto thee, Arise and take up thy bed and go thy way into thine house.' And immediately he arose, took up the bed, and went forth before them all; insomuch that they were all amazed, and glorified God, saying, We never saw it on this fashion."

Now, we have here a beautiful illustration of the evidential place of a miracle. Jesus admits that only God can forgive sins, and the argument of His miracle may be thus stated: "It is true that none can forgive sins but God; but it is also true that none can heal the paralytic by a word but God; if, therefore, I do that latter work before your eyes, you have a proof that I am entitled to perform that other work, the forgiveness of sins, whose performance lies in a department beyond the range of your inspection. The two things, each in its own province, are alike the prerogatives of Deity; and, by the manifestation of the one, I give you the confirmation of my claim to the exercise of the other." But what is true of this one miracle, in its relation to the claim that Jesus had power on earth to forgive sins, is true of the miracles of Christ as a whole in their relation to all the claims which He ever advanced.* This is abundantly evident from the following passages which have been already before us: "The works that I do in my Father's name bear witness of me. If I do not the works of my Father, believe me not; but if I do, though you believe not me, believe the works, that ye may know and believe that the Father is in me and I in him. If I had not done among them the works which none other man did, they had not had sin. Believest thou not that I am in the Father and the Father in me? The words that I speak unto you I speak not of myself; but the Father that dwelleth in me, he doeth the works. Believe me that I am in the Father and the Father in me, or else believe me for the very works' sake."†

---

* So Canon Westcott, in his weighty work on "The Gospel of the Resurrection," says, p. 174: "It may indeed be said that the Resurrection (of Christ) is the historic seal of the Incarnation, which remains forever a mystery, removed from witness."

† John x. 25, 37, 38; xv. 24; xiv. 10, 11.

Now, putting together all these words of the Lord Jesus, it is most evident that they imply the following things; namely, that there was in the person, words, character, and conduct of the Lord, enough to lead men to believe that He is in the Father and the Father in Him; that for the sake of those who could not arrive by one step at such a conclusion, the miracles were provided as the Father's visible testimony to His claims; that, even if there were no other evidence than that given by the miracles, men ought to hear and believe Him simply on the ground of the witness which they bore to Him, or "for the very works' sake;" and that, if, in the face of such evidence as the miracles bore to Him, men should reject Him, they would be guilty of aggravated and inexcusable sin.

A similar deduction as to the evidential value of the miracles must be drawn from the language of Peter on the day of Pentecost, when he spoke of Jesus to his hearers as "a man approved of God among them by miracles and wonders and signs, which God did by him in the midst of them as they themselves also knew;"* and from the words of the author of the Epistle to the Hebrews, when he says: "How shall we escape if we neglect so great salvation, which at first began to be spoken by the Lord, and was con-

---

* Acts ii. 22.

firmed unto us by them that heard him; God also bearing them witness; both with signs and wonders and with divers miracles and gifts of the Holy Ghost, according to his own will."*

Clearly, therefore, in the New Testament, the miracles, over and above any other significance that they may possess, are regarded as God's attestation and confirmation of the claims of those at whose word they were performed, and as thereby also sealing to us the truth of the doctrines, which, in connection with them, were taught. When Jesus showed the woman of Samaria that He had a full knowledge of her personal history, though He had never met her on the earth before, she rightly concluded that He was a prophet ; and that prepared her for accepting as true the statement which He made, when, in answer to her reference to the Messiah, He said, "I, that speak unto thee, am he." Reasoning from similar premises, we come to a similar conclusion, and affirm that the miracles, when themselves proved to be real, do, in their turn, attest the truthfulness of the claims put forth by Jesus, and so affix to all His statements the official and authoritative seal of God.

Against all this, however, it has been contended by some earnest Christians, that so far from confirming the claims of those at whose word they were per-

---

* Hebrews ii. 4.

formed, and attesting the doctrines which they taught, the miracles must first be themselves tested by the doctrines, before they can be received as from God, and regarded as of any value. The claims and doctrines, it is alleged, must be judged entirely on spiritual grounds, and the miracles are to be received because of their connection with the doctrines, rather than the doctrines because of their connection with the miracles. It may be well, therefore, to enter somewhat fully into the consideration of this subject, the rather that since the days of Coleridge, and very much owing to the influence exerted by him on modern theological enquiry, there has been a tendency among many to adopt opinions which, when fairly carried out, would, in my view, make the evidential value of miracles a vanishing quantity, and ultimately reduce it to a nonentity.

Let us concede, here, that the claims of Jesus and the doctrines which He taught are true, altogether independently of the miracles. The miracles did not make them true; but they helped to make their truth more manifest. Take the case of a man accused of a crime. Either he is innocent or guilty from the very first; yet evidence is led; and the effect is to make plain which of the two he is. So, again, in mathematics, every proposition in Euclid is true independently of its demonstration. The demonstration only makes its truth apparent. Similarly,

Jesus is of God, and His doctrines are true altogether independently of the miracles He wrought; and the miracles are true altogether independently of the doctrines; but the truth of the miracles makes that of His claims and His doctrines more evident, and for that reason miracles were performed at the inauguration of the Gospel.

Again, let us admit, that in the age of the Apologists, and during the English deistical controversy, attention was, by many, too exclusively devoted to the department of the external evidences, while that of the experimental was, to a large extent, neglected. Yet, that affords no proper reason why we should now ignore the external evidences altogether. There are external evidences, and there are experimental evidences. Each species has its own province, and each is to be taken in its own order, and estimated at its own value. There is a divine adaptation in the doctrines of the Gospel to the wants and condition of the human heart, and in seeking to establish the truth of Christianity, that must not, by any means, be lost sight of, any more than we should forget the glorious effects which have resulted from the belief of the Gospel wherever it has been made known. But neither, on the other hand, must we, ourselves, ignore, or suffer others to make light of, the attestation of the claims of Jesus, which was given by God in the miracles which He wrought. We do not put the miracles in the place of Christian experience, but neither must we allow Christian experience to cast the miracles entirely into the shade. In the line of proof, the miracles come first, introducing the messenger from heaven; then on the ground of that divine testimony which they bore to Him, we believe His teaching and receive Himself; and after that, His teaching having been believed, experience begins to bear its witness. Reverting to the case of the woman of Samaria, it was the evidence given by her to the people of her city regarding His miraculous knowledge of her history, that induced them to go out to Jesus; but after they had been with Him, they came back, saying: "Now we believe, not because of thy saying, for we have heard Him ourselves, and know that this is, indeed, the Christ, the Saviour of the world." That is to say, they had now additional evidence, besides that of the miracle to which she bore testimony, and from their own experience in their interview with Him, they were sure that He was the Messiah. But it must not be supposed that the miracle was of no value to them, though they put their later experience above it; on the contrary, but for it, and the woman's testimony to it, they would never have gone out to meet Him. Now, similarly, with ourselves; if we have attained to the evidence of inward experience, or if we have any right idea of the grandeur of the effects which have been produced on men, on society, and on the world at large, through the ministry and the Gospel of Christ, we shall, unquestionably, put both of these above the testimony which is borne to Him by the miracles that were wrought during His life upon the earth; but we are not at liberty to say that these miracles have not helped us up to the experience which we thus so highly prize. On the contrary, they were a step, and a very important step too, in the ladder up which we have ascended to the privileged height on which now we stand. It is most unwise to set one branch of evidence up against another, as some writers have done here; and if, in the remarks which I am now to make, I shall be led to speak almost exclusively of the worth of the miracles, and to take high ground on that, let it not be supposed that in order thereto, I seek to lower the value of the evidence of experience—I wish only to give to each its due.

By far the ablest exponent of the view which I am now to controvert, is Dr. Trench, the present Archbishop of Dublin; and that I may not misrepresent his opinions, I shall quote a few sentences from two of the chapters of the Preliminary Essay, prefixed to his valuable "Notes on the Miracles of our Lord." His words are these: "A miracle does not prove the truth of a doctrine, or the divine mission of Him that brings it to pass. That which alone it claims for Him at the first, is the right to be listened to; it puts Him in the alternative of coming from heaven or from hell.

The doctrine must first commend itself to the conscience as being good, and only then can the miracle seal it as divine. But the first appeal is from the doctrine to the moral nature of man."* Again: "It may be objected, if this be so, if there be this inward witness of the truth, what need then of the miracle? to what end does it serve when the truth has accredited itself already? It has, indeed, accredited itself as good, as from God in the sense that all which is good and true is from Him, as whatever was precious in the teaching even of the heathen sage or poet was from Him, but not yet as a new word directly from Him, a new speaking on His part to man. The miracles are to be the credentials for the bearer of that good word, signs that He has a special mission for the realization of the purpose of God in regard to humanity."† Once more: "Are then, it may be asked, the miracles to occupy no place at all in the array of proofs for the certainty of the things which we have believed? On the contrary, a most important place. We should greatly miss them if they did not appear in sacred history, if we could not point to them there; for they belong to the very idea of a Redeemer, which would remain most incomplete without them. We could not, ourselves, without having that idea infinitely weakened and impoverished, conceive of Him as not doing such

---

* Trench's "Notes on the Miracles," p. 24.   † Ibid., p. 24.

works; and those to whom we presented Him as a Lord and Saviour might very well answer, Strange that one should come to deliver men from the bondage of nature which was crushing them, and yet Himself have been subject to its heaviest laws; Himself wonderful, and yet His appearance accompanied by no analogous wonders in nature; claiming to be the life, and yet Himself powerless in the encounter with death; however much He promised in word, never realizing any part of His promise in deed; giving nothing in hand, no first-fruits of power, no pledges of great things to come." "They would have a right to ask, Why did He give no signs that He came to connect the visible with the invisible world? Why did He do nothing to break the yoke of custom and experience, nothing to show men that the constitution which He pretended to reveal has a true foundation."*

Now, there is here not a little of that "luminous haze" which we so often find in those who drank at the well of Coleridge, and it is a little difficult to seize the precise thought which he designs to express. Yet when we look minutely at his words, we shall find that they are inconsistent not only with the Scriptural view which I have already set before you, but also with his own exposition of one of the miracles on which he has commented in the body of his work.

---

* Ibid., p. 93.

I may best expose the erroneous nature of his view in a series of observations on it.

First, it is quite inconsistent with the clear meaning of the Saviour's words, which I have already quoted. Again and again, as we have seen, the Lord claimed to be received "for the very works' sake;" and on one very solemn occasion He declared that the guilt of the Jews was greatly aggravated by the fact, that He had done such miracles in the midst of them.

Now, how could Jesus have spoken after such a fashion, if His supernatural works claimed for Him, at first, only the right to be listened to? He did not blame the Jews for not listening to Him, neither did He find fault with them, because after hearing His words, they still refused to acknowledge His works as divine; but His charge was that they did not receive or believe Him as the Messiah; and He declared that in rejecting Him they were guilty of aggravated sin, because the works which He did, clearly proved Him to be from the Father.

But in all this, on Trench's principle, Jesus was laying a stress on the miracles which they were not able to bear, and weakening His cause by basing His claim to acceptance on purely objective grounds. Surely there must be something wrong with a theory which, in its sweeping results, would blame the Master for asking to be believed "for the very works' sake."

Secondly, this mode of viewing the miracles is inconsistent with the Archbishop's own explanation of the evidential value of the miracle of the healing of the paralytic, in the body of his book. Here is his comment on the conversation between Jesus and His antagonists on that occasion : " They," (that is, the spectators when they said, " This man blasphemeth : who can forgive sins but God only?") "were murmuring, no doubt, within themselves. These honors are easily snatched ; any pretender may go about the world claiming this power, and saying to this man and that, 'Thy sins be forgiven thee ;' but where is the evidence that his word is allowed and ratified in heaven, that this which is spoken on earth is sealed in heaven ? In the very nature of the power which this man asserts for himself, he is secure from detection ; for this releasing of a man from the condemnation of his sins is an act wrought in the inner spiritual world, attested by no outer and visible sign ; therefore it is easily claimed, since it cannot be disproved." And our Lord's answer, meeting this evil thought in their hearts is, in fact, this : " You accuse me, that I am claiming a safe power, since in the very nature of the benefit bestowed no sign follows, nothing to show whether I have challenged it rightfully or not. I will therefore put myself to more decisive proof. I will speak a word and I will claim a power—which if I claim falsely, I shall be con-

188   EVIDENTIAL VALUE OF THE MIRACLES.

vinced upon the instant to be an impostor and a deceiver. I will say to this sick man, 'Rise up and walk;' by the effects as they follow or do not follow, you may judge whether I have a right to say unto him, Thy sins be forgiven thee."* Here, then, is one case in which the miracle did prove, on the Archbishop's own showing, the truth of the claim put forth by Him who wrought it. But if, in one instance, his principle must be set aside, can it be received at all? This act of healing was something more than a claiming of the right to be listened to, or a putting of Jesus in the alternative of coming from heaven or from hell. It was an attestation by that which was submitted to men's eyes, of His right and power to do that which in its very nature lay out of the region of proof.

Moreover, the doctrine here had not to commend itself as good, before the miracle could seal it as divine. The scribes were undoubtedly right in their belief that God alone can forgive sin. That, as an abstract proposition, is a good doctrine, and, if they were bound to test the miracle by that alone before receiving it, then they would have been blameless in rejecting it. But to this, perhaps, Dr. Trench would reply, that the miracle in this case proclaims it to be a new word directly from God, that Jesus, as the Son

---

* Trench's "Notes on the Miracles," pp. 205, 206.

of Man, had power on earth to forgive sin. Unfortunately, however, he has laid it down, as a principle, that the doctrine cannot be authenticated as a new word by the miracle, until it has first been received as a true word by the conscience. Now, on the very surface of the narrative it appears that the miracle, in this case, was wrought, not after the doctrine was received as good and true, but for the purpose of convincing all present of its truth; for before He spoke to the paralytic, the Lord said that He did it "that they might know that the Son of man hath power on earth to forgive sin." Here, therefore, the first appeal was not to the moral nature, but to the miracle, and the supernatural work was done to confirm the claims of the Messiah and authenticate the words which He spake. The Archbishop's theory, therefore, breaks down in his own hands, as far as this miracle is concerned, and so we may justly question its truth in the case of the others.

But thirdly, I object to the view of Dr. Trench and the school to which he belongs, because it gives a changing value to the miracle, according to the time at which it is regarded. At first, the supernatural work is viewed as only a call to attention; then when the doctrine is approved by the conscience, the miracle becomes a divine attestation of the doctrine as a "new" word from God. Now this is a most unsatisfactory way of treating the subject. What a miracle is, I maintain it must be always. It stands on its own foundation, and is to be judged by its own tests; and if received as genuine, its testimony is distinct, determinate, and constant; not one thing now, and another again. If it do not at first attest the doctrine as from God, it cannot afterward; if it confirm the divinity of the doctrine at all, it must do so from the first and always. Such a method of dealing with it as the Archbishop has adopted, must end in making it prove nothing. "If," as Dr. Wardlaw says, "so far as the miracle is concerned, the message which it accompanies may be from hell as well as from heaven; from the devil as well as from God; from the kingdom of lies no less than from the kingdom of truth; if the miracle implies no more than a right to be listened to, having nothing in it at all evidential of the source from which the message comes, it is not easy to see how it can become evidential of this, after that source has been ascertained, from the nature of the message itself. If it is not proof at first of the message being from God, it cannot be proof afterward. It may, if you will, be regarded as attesting its being 'a new word,' but not as attesting a new word from Him, a new speaking on His part to man. That is determined by the character of the message itself; as attested by man's conscience or moral nature. The miracle attests nothing. It may be a diabolical sign just as really and as much as a divine one. It is solely the nature of the doctrine that certifies its origin, not the miracle at all. The theory, as it appears to me, divests miracles of their evidential value entirely."* This difficulty seems to have been felt by Dr. Trench himself, for once and again, he asks: "Are the miracles to occupy no place in the array of proofs?" and then having given them, in one sentence, a subjective value as belonging to the very idea of a Redeemer, he oscillates back to the old view, by admitting that if there were no miracles men would be justified in saying of Jesus, "Why did He give no signs that He came to connect the visible with the invisible world? Strange that one should come, Himself wonderful, and yet His appearance accompanied by no analogous wonders in nature!" But what is this, if it be not a craving for some external attestation or sign of the wonderful mission? What is this but asking some evidence, by means of the supernatural that is seen, of the truth of that claim to the supernatural in a province that is unseen and lies out of the region of investigation. The more we ponder these somewhat hazy sentences, the more are we disposed to ask, Can it be that the miracles have such an impalpable value as evidences to Jesus and His Gospel, that we cannot shape it into distinctness? Is it possible that

---

* Wardlaw on "Miracles," pp. 215, 216.

works to which our Lord so clearly appealed in attestation of His mission, should, like a dissolving view, pass while we gaze upon them, from one thing into another, and finally disappear, leaving nothing behind? It would be a poor exchange for the definiteness of the ground taken by the apostles on this point, to accept the uncertainty of that which has here been substituted.

Fourthly. This theory is unsatisfactory, inasmuch as the appeal which it makes to the moral nature of man must ever be a most uncertain and, therefore, a very useless criterion. I admit most cheerfully that the truth of God does commend itself to the moral nature of man, by its adaptation to his circumstances and wants; but that is a very different thing from making the conscience, depraved as it is, the standard by which all that claims to be truth coming from God is to be tried. Why was an external revelation needed by man at all, if it were not to give him a certain for an uncertain standard? But precisely as there was need for an external revelation to be a standard of truth, there was need that the revelation itself should in some external way convince us of its genuineness; and this is done by miracles. 'If men are left to their own preferences, these, as all history before the advent proves, will be as numerous as the dialects of Babel. We need some external stamp of authority which will authenticate some messenger from God, and give us a reason, independent of, and in addition to, the character of His utterances, for giving heed to His words, and we find that in miracles.

Fifthly. This theory of the Archbishop is based on what seems to me, at least, the erroneous opinion that true miracles may be performed in attestation of falsehood. Immediately preceding the extracts already given from his essay, the following statement will be found: "This fact, however, that the kingdom of lies has its wonders, no less than the kingdom of truth, would be alone sufficient to convince us that miracles cannot be appealed to absolutely and simply, in proof of the doctrine which the worker of them proclaims; and God's word (Deut. xiii. 5) expressly declares the contrary."* But a little before,† he had said that the works of anti-Christ and his organs, are not "miracles in the very highest sense of the word; they only in part partake of the essential elements of the miracles." Now, if this be so, surely the conclusion to be drawn from the fact, if it be a fact, that the kingdom of lies has its wonders as well as the kingdom of truth, ought to be, not that a miracle purely and simply cannot prove a doctrine; but that only "miracles in the very highest sense of the term" (as all through we have been using it) and possessing all the essential elements of the mira-

---

* "Notes on the Miracles," *ubi supra*, pp. 23, 24.   † Ibid., 23.

cle, do absolutely and simply prove a doctrine. The amount of the argument here, therefore, is simply to put us on our guard against being imposed upon by miracles which are not miracles in the highest sense of the term, and to bid us, before implicitly receiving the doctrine on the faith of the miracle, be sure that it is a miracle indeed. Dr. Trench here touches the subject of the criterion by which miracles are to be tested, and not at all the evidential value of those which, on right grounds, are received as works of God. Thus far, granting his premises, the argument will carry us: Doubtful miracles are not to be relied on any more than doubtful arguments; therefore we must be on the watch lest we receive false miracles as true.

But can we fully admit his premises? Is it the case that miracles, in any proper sense of the word, have been wrought by evil spirits, or by the organs of anti-Christ in support of error? In answer to that question it might be enough to say with Mansell: "It remains yet to be shown that in all human experience, any instance can be produced of a real miracle wrought by evil spirits for the purposes of deception;" but to content myself with that would perhaps leave room for the insinuation that I shrink from an investigation of the passages of Scripture which are generally supposed to bear upon this point. Let me, therefore, ask you to look with me for a little at the more important of them. These are the chapters in the beginning of Exodus, relating to the works of the Egyptian magicians; and the verses in Deuteronomy referred to by Dr. Trench in the extract already quoted. Let us examine them both.

First, As to the wonders performed by the magicians. From a careful study of the chapters to which I have referred, the following things may be gathered; namely, that the magicians could only go a certain length in their reproductions, or rather, as I judge it to have been, their imitations of the works of Moses; that on all the occasions on which they were successful, intimation had been given by Moses of what he was about to do in time to allow opportunity on their part for preparation; that in the case in which they failed no intimation of his intention had been given beforehand by Moses, and so they were taken unawares, and had no preparation made; and, finally, that they never attempted to remove the plagues which came at the word of Moses, but contented themselves with appearing to produce, on a small scale and to a very limited extent, effects similar to those which were wrought at Moses' word. Now, does not all this look as if, throughout, they had been working with simply natural agents? and that, when they failed, they did so because they were taken by surprise and had no opportunity to study how they were to appear to rival this new manifestation of the hand of God? Indeed, if this explanation be not accepted, it will be hard to see what there was more difficult of performance for them in the bringing of the gnats, than in the production of the frogs. Nay, if it be allowed that they really and truly changed a rod into a serpent, which was a virtual impartation of life and organization to a piece of matter, it will be impossible to explain why they should have been baffled by anything. Hence, putting all these things together, we are compelled to conclude that the wonders done by the magicians were not miracles at all, but mere feats of legerdemain similar to those which are common to this day among the jugglers of the East.

But some will say, Is it not affirmed that "the magicians did so?" and does not that imply that they did the same things as Moses? No, we reply; for in the instance in which they failed, the same words are used: "the magicians did so, and they could not." What to me is conclusive on the point, however, is that some of the things done at the word of Moses were virtual creations; and it is inconceivable that God should delegate to evil spirits, or to men, such a power as was needed for the performance of such works, for the mere purpose of contending with Himself; as if one in a game of chess should match his right hand against his left. The thing is preposterous. Clearly, therefore, whatever these works of the magicians were, they were not miracles in the only sense in which we can employ the word.

But neither is there any foundation for the view of Trench in the passage in Deuteronomy to which he has referred. The words are these: "If there arise among you a prophet, or a dreamer of dreams, and giveth thee a sign, or a wonder, and the sign or the wonder come to pass, whereof he spake unto thee, saying, Let us go after other gods, which thou hast not known, and let us serve them; thou shalt not hearken unto the words of that prophet, or that dreamer of dreams; for the Lord your God proveth you, to know whether ye love the Lord God with all your heart and with all your soul. Ye shall walk after the Lord your God, and fear him, and keep his commandments, and obey his voice, and ye shall serve him, and cleave unto him. And that prophet, or that dreamer of dreams, shall be put to death; because he hath spoken to turn you away from the Lord your God, which brought you out of the land of Egypt, and redeemed you out of the house of bondage, to thrust thee out of the way which the Lord thy God commanded thee to walk in: so shalt thou put the evil away from the midst of thee."* Now, let us remember that this passage is adduced to prove that the first appeal is from the doctrine to the moral

---

* Deut. xiii. 1–5.

nature of man, because the kingdom of lies has its wonders as well as the kingdom of truth. But a little investigation will convince any one that the appeal here is not to the moral nature of man at all, but to the consistency of God himself. The Hebrews had already received a revelation miraculously attested from God, and the argument is that as God cannot deny or contradict Himself, any wonders or signs wrought in opposition to the precepts of that revelation are to be regarded as impostures, and the workers of them are to be punished as having been guilty of high treason against the theocratic king. The case is not that of a people to whom miracles are presented for the first time; but rather that of those who had themselves seen the giving of the manna, the bringing of water out of the rock, and the leading of the tribes by the pillar of cloud and flame. Now, as their law had been thus unequivocally established by God, they were not to allow themselves to be moved from it by anything else, no matter how marvellous, to outward appearance, might be the signs and wonders by which its advocates enforced it. And so, as I have said, the appeal, here, is not to the moral nature of man at all, but to the consistency of God; and it makes the doctrines only a test of miracle, *after they have themselves been received as miraculously attested, and so from God.*

It may be said, however, that if a previous external

revelation, miraculously confirmed, ought to be thus employed to try the miracles of those who might afterward arise, and pretend to work them for the purpose of turning men away from it; then, by parity of reasoning, the prior revelation which God has made of Himself in the heart of man should be employed to test the doctrines of the divine messenger, and through them the miracles which He professes to perform; so that thus we are brought back to the old appeal to the moral nature of man. But we must distinguish between things that differ. In the case supposed by Moses, the pretender to miraculous power seeks to oppose and draw men away from truth, which they have already received on good evidence as divine; whereas, in the other case, he is adducing his supernatural works as witnesses of the divinity of some new truth, not contradicting that which they have already received, but so far transcending it as to be above the reach of their discovery. In this last instance, the miracle-worker takes his stand upon admitted and accepted truth, and seeks to lead men up to some new and higher principles, the miracle being not a witness to the old which they have already received, but to the new which he desires them to accept. If he controverts the old, then the law laid down by Moses may come into operation; but if he simply builds upon it, and seeks only to rise above it, then most evidently the old received truth cannot be made a test of any kind, wherewith to try the miracle by which he confirms the new. The miracles are not wrought by him in support of natural religion, or of those truths which may be gathered from the moral nature of man; but in confirmation of new truths which he is bringing to light. Hence, it must be evident at a glance, that in a case of this sort, the old truths of natural religion, admitted and acted upon as they are by both parties, are comparatively worthless as tests, either of the miracles or of the new truths revealed in connection with them. In the case of the Scriptures, indeed, the harmony of their doctrines with the moral nature of man is one of the proofs of their truth; but it is not on that alone that the value of the evidence of miracles depends. They have their own distinct and independent place. They stand upon a footing of their own; and if they be received as divine, then since they postulate the truths of natural theology, and do not controvert them, the natural theologian has only to listen to and believe the revelation which they introduce.

But I need not pursue this subject further, since I have said enough to convince you of the unsatisfactory and untenable nature of the view maintained by the eminent prelate to whom I have referred. Nor would I have dwelt so long upon his argument, if it had not been that the weight of his great ability; the influence of his deservedly high position; and the

EVIDENTIAL VALUE OF THE MIRACLES. 201

gratitude which all biblical students owe to him, for the valuable assistance they have received from his writings, are apt to induce many to accept his reasonings without due examination. His error seems to me to be, that he has mistaken the ultimate estimate of the miracles to which the Christian world has attained for that which was entertained at first by enquirers coming toward Christianity, but not yet believers in its truth. There is a sense in which it is correct to say that "the true revelation is one of mutual interdependence, the miracles proving the doctrines, and the doctrines approving the miracles, and both held together for us in blessed unity in the person of Him who spake the words and did the works;" but that is after the truth of both have been, each on its own proper grounds, received. It may be true, also, that in looking on the doctrines as throwing back light on the miracles, we are receiving "the sum total of the impression which this divine revelation is intended to make on us, instead of taking an impression only partial and one-sided;" but it is equally true, that this sum total has come to us as the aggregate of two different instalments. We do not maintain that the miracles are the sole evidences on which our holy religion rests. Neither are we prepared to affirm that they furnish that sort of testimony which is most likely to move the mind of this generation; but what we contend for is, that when their genuineness

9*

is admitted, they do give divine attestation to the claims and doctrines of Him at whose word they were wrought; and, for that contention, we have the example and the warrant of the Lord Jesus Christ himself.

Thus have I sought to outline for you both of those arguments which, in my second lecture, I foreshadowed. By the one we were led to infer the Divine Personality of Christ, from the character He manifested, the words He spake, and the influence which His life has had on the history of humanity. Then, that Personality accepted, His miracles cease to present any difficulty, as being only the accompanying halo of that grander miracle which He is Himself. By the other, having established the credibility of the miracles, against all objections, we have found that they give an infallible endorsement to the claims made by Him, and in connection with which He wrought them. The two methods are related to each other much as the proof of the correctness of a sum is to the sum itself. The scholar works out his problem one way; then, taking the answer, he begins on that, and reverses all his operations, until he ends where he began. In the first argument, reaching the Personality of Christ on independent grounds, we hang the miracles on that; in the second, we rise through the miracles to the perception of Christ's Divine Personality. Nothing proved by the one, is taken for granted in the other. They are distinct and independent, yet both alike lead to the conclusion that Jesus Christ is the " Word made flesh," or as Paul has otherwise expressed the same truth, "God manifest in the flesh." But if this be so, what then? Can we stop there without going further? Nay, for if these two lines of proof be conclusive, then it must follow that the Lord Jesus Christ is not only a Saviour, but the only possible Saviour; and so a keen edge is given to the question, " How shall we escape if we neglect so great salvation?"

Will you forgive me, if now quitting the argumentative style to which throughout these discourses I have studiously confined myself, I make one personal appeal, and beseech you to consider the choice which is thus set before you—salvation through the reception of the crucified, but divinely attested Son of God, or as the punishment of rejecting Him, "everlasting destruction from the presence of the Lord and from the glory of His power." Take heed how you decide between these alternatives, for it is your ETERNITY that trembles in the balance. Beware, I beseech you, of the guilt and doom of those of whom the Lord himself thus spoke: " If I had not come and spoken unto them, they had not had sin; but now they have no cloak for their sin. He that hateth me hateth my Father also. If I had not done among them the works that none other man did, they had not had sin; but now they have both seen and hated both me and my Father."

THE SPIRITUAL SIGNIFICANCE OF THE MIRACLES.

LECTURE VII.

THE SPIRITUAL SIGNIFICANCE OF THE MIRACLES.

John ii. 11 : This beginning of miracles did Jesus in Cana of Galilee, and manifested forth his glory.

THE term sign, which in the New Testament is so frequently used in connection with the miracles of Christ, has three distinct meanings. It denotes, in its simplest usage, a means of identification, as when the angel said to the shepherds, "This shall be a sign unto you,"* and then proceeded to describe the circumstances in which the infant Jesus would be found by them; or as when Paul, referring to his autographic endorsement of his second letter to the Thessalonians, uses these words: "The salutation of Paul with mine own hand, which is the token (σημεῖον, sign) in every epistle; so I write."† It designates, again, a proof or evidence, furnished by one set of facts, to the reality and genuineness of another; as when Paul alleges in writing to the Corinthians‡ that "the signs of an apostle were wrought among them;" meaning thereby that the patience, the signs, and

---

* Luke ii. 12.   † 2 Thess. iii. 17.   ‡ 2 Cor. xii. 12.

wonders, and mighty deeds which they saw, conclusively authenticated him as an apostle, since only an apostle was in a position to manifest them. But it signifies also, in the third place, a symbol or emblem, as when Ezekiel* gave a sign to the house of Israel by the type of a siege; or by digging through the wall and carrying out thereby his baggage as the baggage of one going forth into captivity. Now the miracles of Jesus Christ were signs in all these three senses. They identified Him as the Messiah foretold in prophecy; they authenticated Him as the Son of God, and furnished evidence of the truth of the claims which He put forth; and they were emblems in the material sphere, of the blessings which He came to bestow in the spiritual, and of the manner in which they were to be received by those whom He designed to benefit.

In our former lectures, however, we have viewed them almost exclusively as identifications and authentications; and it may serve to give something like completeness to our consideration of the subject, as well as to bring us for a season out of the region of discussion and debate, if to-day we restrict our attention to the spiritual significance of the miracles of Christ.

These wondrous works are not only the seals by

---

* Ezekiel iv. 3.

which the revelation made by Jesus is attested as from God, but they are themselves a part of that revelation. They have in themselves, in the circumstances in connection with which they were wrought, and in the manner in which they were performed, much that reveals the heart of God unto us, and enables us to understand how we are to receive at His hands the priceless blessings of regeneration and salvation. By His miracles, no less than by His words and by His conduct, Jesus showed the Father unto us. They were signs not only as indicating the source, but also as symbolizing the nature of the new life which He came to impart to men. And it is not difficult to see the philosophy that lies beneath this view of them. We commonly think of them, indeed, as manifestations of the Divine power; but the attributes of Deity are so inseparable in their unity, and so harmonious in their operation, that we can never see only one of them at a time. Always they are manifested together, so that no matter which of them may be for the moment most apparent, the others are sure to make their presence also known. If love be pre-eminent, somewhere we may be sure justice will be seen qualifying or conditioning its manifestation; if justice be in the foreground, then, if we look attentively, we shall see love also at hand. So when God puts forth His power in the miracle, we always perceive something more than power—something which reveals to us the character of Him whose the power is, and lets us see more clearly into the meaning of His dealings with us. We cannot have the light of the sun without its heat; and we cannot perceive the omnipotence of the miracles without at the same time discovering the merciful purpose of that Gospel in connection with which they were wrought.

Jesus Christ came to earth to work the great miracle of man's redemption. That was His dominating aim; but in moving toward that, He gave out of the fulness of His benevolence, and as a kind of alms to those around Him, the minor miracles of which the gospels have preserved the record; and each of these is, in its own department, and from its own angle, a miniature of the one great miracle which He is continually working in the regeneration of the human soul. As the tree repeats itself in the framework of every leaf that hangs upon its branches, so the one great miracle which Christ came to perform, is reproduced in some sort in each of His miracles; though, from the nature of the case, no one of them can give us a full idea of His work, and it is only when we put them all together that we have anything like a complete representation of all that He has done for humanity. Each of them is patterned after some one aspect of His great mediatorial and redemptive work; and by studying them all we may come to a better apprehension both of it and of Him.

Moreover, we must not forget here that marvellous correspondence which God has made between the outer and the inner, between the material and the spiritual, which lies at the foundation of all reasoning from analogy, which gives its power to the parable, and which makes a pertinent and telling illustration more potent than any argument. The external is but the visible image of the internal, and the poet was not wrong when he proposed the question:

> "What if earth
> Be but the shadow of heaven, and things therein
> Each to the other like, more than on earth is thought?"

When, therefore, Christ puts forth His supernatural power in the sphere of material things and on the plane of common life, we may be sure that we have in that a type of His working in the sphere of grace, and in the spiritual domain. He uses the seen to help us to the apprehension of the unseen; and thus each of His miracles becomes also a parable, and is, to those who have the eye to see it, luminous with instruction in the nature of His Gospel, and the things of His kingdom. In the Palazzo Rospigliosi, at Rome, Guido's famous painting of Aurora is on the ceiling, and therefore the visitor cannot examine it without much discomfort and great disadvantage; but a mirror has been placed in the room at such an angle as to present a reflection of the picture to the spectator at a point where he can conveniently study it at leisure. So the great miracle of the renewing of the soul is above our inspection; but in the minor miracles wrought by Jesus on men and nature, we have manifold reflections—as in a mirror—of that transcendent spiritual work, and these help us to the better understanding of that. In the words of Steinmeyer, "As a parable shows on earthly grounds the reflex of a higher truth, in order to serve as a means of explaining the latter, so a miracle which relieves an earthly pain is the symbol of the help within reach for a deeper need. Our Lord cures the sick of the palsy; but the first words of the narrative point most expressly to a higher region. He gives sight to him that was born blind; but the concluding words of the history exclude the thought of a mere deed of compassion."*

Fully to illustrate this view of the significance of the Gospel miracles, would require us to take up and give a separate exposition of each of them. But that is evidently out of the question now, and so referring you to Trench's Notes, which in this regard are of pre-eminent value,† I content myself with the mention of a few general characteristics of the miracles of Christ, when viewed thus, as a part of His revelation of God's Gospel to men.

---

* "The Miracles of our Lord in Relation to Modern Criticism," by F. L. Steinmeyer, p. 46.
† See Appendix, Note D.

I begin with the obvious fact that they are all miracles of Benevolence. They illustrate the love that is at the centre of the Gospel; and they show in their own way, that "God sent not his Son into the world to condemn the world, but that the world, through him, might be saved." "Jesus of Nazareth went about doing good." His mission was to bring His Divine love to bear upon the miseries and weaknesses of men. He healed the sick; He cleansed the lepers; He opened the eyes of the blind, and unstopped the ears of the deaf; He made the lame to walk, and the dumb to speak, and the dead to live. He brought down no fire from heaven to consume His adversaries; and when His too impetuous apostles suggested such a course, He was ready with the reply, "Ye know not what manner of spirit ye are of; for the Son of Man is not come to destroy men's lives, but to save them" —a reply which indicated that, as I have just been saying, He subordinated the power in His miracles to the loving purpose of His ministry as a whole.

Now, in regard to His performance of these miracles, two things are apparent, namely: first, that He was sometimes Himself the prime mover in the matter, and came unasked to the help of the sufferer; and, second, that He never refused to perform a miracle at the entreaty of the afflicted or their friends. He was sometimes, to adopt the language of the prophet, "found of them that sought him not;" but always they who did seek Him found Him, if only they sought Him "with all their heart and with all their mind." And it is thus also with the better blessings of His salvation. Some, like the blind man, of whom we read in the ninth chapter of John, are healed spiritually almost before they ask to be healed at all. The Lord has seen them and has had compassion on them. But to keep us from murmuring at that, or rebelling against His sovereignty, there comes in the other fact, that all who really ask for healing are sure to obtain it; and if you want to know how to apply for deliverance at His hands, read these narratives and see how, in the days of his flesh, Bartimeus cried to Him for his sight; and the lepers came to Him to be cleansed; and the Syrophœnician woman made entreaty with Him for her daughter, then go, and do ye likewise; and go at once, for Jesus of Nazareth passeth by, and if you let Him go past altogether, you must remain not only unblessed, but positively blighted.

For there is one miracle of judgment; though even in that, "mercy rejoiceth against judgment," and when we truly read it we are as much impressed by the love of its manner as by the terror of its matter. I refer, as most of you must be already aware, to the cursing of the barren fig-tree. How paltry and inadequate an explanation of that is given by those who would refer it to an outburst of disappointed temper on the part of the Lord Jesus, I need not stay now to point out to you; for the moment we put it in its true light, all such thoughts regarding it are shamed into insignificance. It is to be read as an appendix to the parable of the barren fig-tree,* and has its key in the fact that such a tree was the recognized symbol of the Jewish nation. The year of grace, which the vineyard-dresser begged in the parable, was now drawing near its close; and still, in spite of its privileges and its foliage, no fruit appeared upon the tree. What was there for it now but the destruction which had then been threatened, and to which, after the lapse of the supplicated delay, the dresser had himself consented? Still, a final warning was to be given, and while the terrible nature of the punishment was indicated in the immediate withering of the tree, the tenderness of the love appears in the fact that the curse fell upon it, and not yet upon the people. "Behold the goodness and severity of God!" On the vegetable product, severity; but toward the people goodness, if haply they might, even at the eleventh hour, be led thereby to repentance, and so saved from the blight which was thus vividly symbolized before their eyes. Let the lesson which the Jews refused to learn not be lost upon us; but while our privileges continue, and our day of grace lasts, let us turn unto

---

* Luke xiii. 6–10.

the Lord with all our hearts and make earnest supplication for His mercy.

But while we note thus the benevolence which was so characteristic of our Lord's supernatural works, let us not fail to recognize also the manner in which that benevolence was manifested, that so we may learn thereby the nature of the Gospel and the extent of its influence. The miracles of Jesus may be divided into three classes. Under the first we range those, constituting the larger number of them, in which He interposed with His divine power for the purpose of arresting disease and giving restoration to health. So far were these from being contrary to nature, that they operated to remedy the unnatural and the abnormal. Disease, in all its forms, is a deviation from man's normal condition; and death is not only non-natural, but anti-natural. But Jesus, in healing the sick, cleansing the lepers, and raising the dead, interposed to bring back the subjects in each case to their true natural condition. He restored each to the normal possession of himself. He brought them all back to health and life, which is the right ideal of physical humanity. Now, precisely in the same way, sin is unnatural to the soul. Depravity is not true spiritual wholeness or health. It is abnormal. It is disease; and by the supernaturalism of His Gospel, as applied to men through the power of the Holy Ghost, the Saviour restores them to their normal spiritual condition. He creates them anew. He healeth all their diseases, because He forgiveth all their iniquities, and bestows upon them that new nature which is the reproduction in them of the image of God, that sin had blighted and defaced. Those that are dead in trespasses and sins, He quickens into newness of life. He raises them up, through His resurrection, so that they set their affections on things that are above. He cleanses them from the leprosy of sin; opens their eyes to behold the wonderful things of His law; unstops their ears to hear His voice; and causes the tongue of the dumb to sing His praise. He is the restorer of humanity to its lost ideal; and gives the man back to himself "redeemed, regenerated, and disenthralled;" so that he may find his "perfect freedom" in the filial service of his God. What a flood of light is cast thus on the work of Christ in its influence on individual men by the contemplation of this class of His supernatural works!

Under the second division of His miracles we range those by which He enlarged and multiplied the existing resources of human happiness. He grafted the supernatural upon the natural, and thereby purified its character and widened its influence. Just as Moses, or rather God through the instrumentality of Moses, provided in the manna a substance closely allied to a natural product of the wilderness, and increased the measure, as well as prolonged the period, of its production; so Jesus, in the miracle of the loaves and fishes, multiplied natural articles of food, and, in that of Cana, heightened the water into wine. Now we have herein a symbol of the influence of the Gospel on human society. That which is already valuable in it, is made more valuable than ever, and is increased so as to become the possession of multitudes, who but for His influence would never have enjoyed it at all. The water of earthly fellowship is transmuted into the wine of spiritual communion; and, in this regard, the very magnitude of the quantity of wine that was miraculously produced, and that has been such a stumbling-block to those who cannot see farther than a favorite theory will allow them, becomes a most interesting and suggestive thing, indicating, as it does, the boundless capacity of the Gospel for ministering to the highest enjoyment of mankind. The bread of ordinary food and the wine of ordinary drink do both alike become sacramental at the miracle-working touch of Jesus, and both alike are lifted by Him into the higher symbolism that links them on to spiritual sustenance and spiritual elevation; so that the one connects itself with the words, "I am the Bread of life," and the other with the expression, "I am the true Vine."* Common things are hallowed for us by the Gospel;

---

* See Appendix, Note E.

SPIRITUAL SIGNIFICANCE OF THE MIRACLES. 219

and the real blessings of human life are by it multiplied and sublimated; that is for us the significance of this class of our Lord's supernatural works.

Under the third division of His miracles, we range those which were evidently designed for the warning or training or testing of His followers. To this belongs the walking of Peter on the waters; which, as even the dullest reader may discover, was a rehearsal in symbol, and therefore a loving warning, of all the incidents connected with that impulsive disciple's over-confidence and denial of his Lord. In the "Bid me come unto thee upon the water," we have the parable of the ejaculation, "Though all men should deny thee, yet will I never deny thee;" in the beginning to sink, we have the prophecy of his fall; in the cry, "Lord, save me, I perish," we have the forecast shadow of the penitential prayer which saved Peter from settling into the despair of Judas; and haply, in the day when the son of Jonas wept those bitter tears, he might feel that if he had taken the hint thus kindly given by his Lord so long before, he might have been saved from the humiliation of his fall; while in the remembrance of the hand held out to catch him as he was going down beneath the waves, there would be to him during these dark days of sorrow the prediction of his ultimate restoration. Both restorations were alike supernatural; and in both alike the love of the Redeemer seeking to train His servant for after-usefulness is conspicuously manifest.

Under this class also we would put the healing of the woman with the issue of blood, and mark, in her case, how a weak faith was nourished into strength, so that she who came with trembling timidity was enabled at the last to tell out before them all everything that was in her heart. Here, too, belong the healing of the Syrophœnician woman's daughter; that of the centurion's servant, and that of Jairus' daughter; the first showing how a strong faith is developed into expression; the second how a mighty faith is rewarded; and the third how an almost expiring confidence is kept burning, and the "bruised reed" is straightened into strength.

And to mention no more, we put in this category also the second miracle of the loaves, whereby the merely carnal among the crowd were winnowed away, and those only remained with Him who, like Peter, could say, "To whom shall we go? Thou hast the words of eternal life, and we believe and are sure that thou art the Christ, the Son of the living God." To borrow the words of another here: This "was a symbolic, didactic, critical miracle. It was meant to teach and also to test, to supply a text for the subsequent sermon, and a touchstone to try the character of those who had followed Jesus with such enthusiasm. The miraculous feast in the wilderness was meant to say to the multitude just what our sacramental feast says to us: 'I, Jesus, the Son of God Incarnate, am the bread of life. What this bread is to your bodies, I myself am to your souls.' And the communicants in that feast were to be tested by the way in which they regarded the transaction. The spiritual would see in it a sign of Christ's divine dignity, and a seal of His saving grace; the carnal would rest simply in the outward fact that they had eaten of the loaves and were filled, and would take occasion from what had happened to indulge in high hopes of temporal felicity under the benign reign of the Prophet and the King who had made His appearance among them."* Thus, by this miracle, and its exposition in the discourse which followed, Jesus did with His adherents what Gideon did with his army when he led them to the brook to drink. He separated the spurious from the true; the carnal from the spiritual.

But what need I more here? I have surely said enough to show you that they who fail to take cognizance of the symbolic purpose of these wondrous works, deprive themselves of the instruction which they were designed to impart.

But I hasten to direct your attention to another peculiarity connected with the miracles of Christ, namely: the fact that faith in Him was needed as a

---

* Alexander Balmain Bruce, D.D., "The Training of the Twelve," p. 120.

prerequisite to the reception of benefit or blessing through them. He never performed them for the satisfaction of curiosity, or for the gratification of those who seemed to wish to put Him to the test of an experiment. During His temptation, Satan sought to induce Him to cast Himself from the pinnacle of the temple—as if to give a sign to the worshippers that thronged its courts, and so bring them flocking around His standard. But He refused to use any such sensational means for the founding of a kingdom which He knew was spiritual. That, however, was not by any means the last time that the same demand was made of Him. The Jews sought after a sign; and repeatedly they asked Him, for their simple gratification, to put forth His supernatural power. But on all such occasions He saw the Satanic spirit revealing itself, and He invariably declined. He knew to what His yielding would have led, even the utter secularizing of His kingdom, and the complete paralysis of His spiritual power—just as in later days the attempt to supply marvels at the popular demand has always ended in undermining the true influence of the Christian Church—and therefore He stood firm. Neither, again, did He perform His miracles in the midst of those, or for the benefit of those, who were antagonistic to Himself. You remember that suggestive saying of Matthew* concerning Nazareth:

---

* Matt. xiii. 58.

"He did not many mighty works there, because of their unbelief;" and the same evangelist tells us that He said to the two blind men in the house, "Believe ye that I am able to do this?"* and that His rule was, "According to your faith be it unto you."† Where there was no faith in Him, no virtue went out of Him; but the poorest suppliant that came to Him with faith, even though it were only as a grain of mustard-seed, departed with the blessing sought.

Now, who does not see how all this illustrates the method in which we become partakers of the blessings of His grace? His salvation is bestowed on "whosoever believeth;" but without faith in Him we derive no blessing from Him. Not on the suspicious, the envious, or the antagonistic does He confer His favors, but only on those who receive Him, and unto them He gives "power to become the sons of God." This is the principle that runs through the administration of His spiritual kingdom; and therefore we are not surprised to find it prominently recognized in works, the performance of which was designed to be symbolical of the manner in which He makes men partakers of His great salvation. But the importance of its recognition, even in these days, will be apparent to all who remember the absurd proposal which was made a few years ago by a medical man

---

* Matt. ix. 28. † Ibid., ix. 29.

of eminence, for the putting of the efficacy of prayer to the test of experiment, by the selection of a ward in an hospital whose patients were to be treated alone by prayer; while those in the other wards were to be left simply and solely to the physicians, without any appeal to God. The very idea of such a test was born out of unbelief. It was as if we should stand by and say, "Let be, and let us see whether there be any God, or any virtue in prayer to Him at all;" and just as Jesus refused in answer to a similar demand to come down from the cross,* so He will always refuse to answer prayer on any such terms. While, on the other hand, as His miracles make constantly apparent, the humble suppliant whose prayer to Him is the child of confidence in Him, and not of suspicion of Him, will never go unblessed. If, therefore, men wish to receive the salvation which He has wrought out for them, let them come in faith to Him, and they will not be sent empty away. The reality of these miracles which He wrought on earth, is a prophecy and a pledge that He is able and willing to give them the spiritual things of which they are the symbols. "Be not afraid, only believe." "All things are possible to him that believeth." These are the sayings which, in this regard, the Gospel miracles make specially emphatic.

---

* Matt. xxvii. 40–43, 49.

But while thus in the working of His miracles the Lord Jesus conditioned the forth-putting of His power on the faith of those who made application for it, we cannot but remark that, within the natural and human sphere, He put the highest honor on the use of means. He never did by miracle what the people were able without miracle to do for themselves. By miracle the dead Lazarus was recalled to life; but before the miracle the stone was rolled away from the cave's mouth; and, after it, the grave clothes were loosed from him; and both by human hands; all to teach us that while the actual recreation of the soul is the work of God, there are some things preparatory to that work which are fairly within the compass of human ability; and some things subsequent to it, and subservient to it, which men must do for themselves, if the newly-imparted life is to have the freest and the fullest play.

Nor is this all; in the impartation of that life itself one may learn from many of the Master's miracles that everything is made to depend on the willinghood of the individual to be blessed, and his attempt to act as if he had already received the blessing. Christ often wrought His cures by issuing commands, obedience to which implied that the cures had already been imparted. Thus He said to the man with the withered arm, "Stretch forth thine hand;" and to the paralytic, "Arise, take up thy bed and walk."

Neither of them had in himself the power to obey. It was their very disease that they had not. Yet each, believing that Jesus was not mocking him, made the attempt, and lo! in the forth-putting of the effort he discovered that the Lord had been beforehand with him and had already conferred on him the cure he sought. Thus, through obedience, which was an evidence of faith, the poor diseased ones received the blessing. And it is the same still in spiritual things. Men often debate which is first in the order of salvation, regeneration or faith? but the whole controversy is about as absurd as if one should ask, Which was first in Lazarus, his restoration to life, or his coming out of the grave? or, Which was first in the paralytic, the reception of his cure, or his rising up and walking? The simple truth is, that in the experience of each, these two things were simultaneous. The cure was obtained in the effort to arise; and the life was made manifest in the coming forth of the dead one from the cave. And from the opposite side, this must be declared, that if the paralytic had not tried to obey the command, he would have had no cure. We cannot tell in any thing where the human agency ceases and the divine begins; and the boundary between the natural and the supernatural, especially in the region of spiritual experience, cannot well be defined. Yet this is always true: God honors faith and obedience;

SPIRITUAL SIGNIFICANCE OF THE MIRACLES. 227

so that we may be certain that if we believe and obey Him, we shall be truly blessed.

But enough. I have said sufficient to convince you that the miracles of Jesus are not mere arbitrary manifestations of power, but are all themselves a part of the revelation which He has given us of the grace of God. They are not "a conglomerate of marvellous anecdotes accidentally heaped together, but parts of a great organic whole, of which every part is in vital coherence with all other."* This is in itself an argument for their reality of no mean force; for the same cannot be said of any other cycles of miracles, save those of which we read in Scripture. But I am speaking of them to-day exegetically, and not apologetically, and in this view of them they are acted parables, having as real and as large a place in the instruction which Christ imparted as that possessed by His discourses themselves. They proclaim His mightiness to save. They reveal the depth of His love. They indicate the manner in which He blesses the souls of men. They give us the assurance that as really as He healed the bodies of those who were afflicted, He will cure our souls; and that as surely as He rose again from the dead, so surely "all that are in their graves shall hear His voice and shall come forth: they that have done good, unto the

---
* Trench, "Notes on the Miracles," p. 40.

resurrection of life, and they that have done evil, unto the resurrection of condemnation."* The outer is the prophecy of the inner, and the conjunct view we have taken of the wondrous works of the Lord, gives new meaning and power to His loving invitation, "Come unto me, all ye that labor and are heavy laden, and I will give you rest."

As I close this series of discourses, which has brought me once more into loving fellowship with the brethren of this Theological faculty, and with you, my dear young friends, who are so soon to go forth as messengers of God's mercy to your fellow-men, there rises up before me a vision of that scene which I have always regarded as one of the most beautiful which any one of the sacred penmen has depicted. "Now, when the sun was setting, all they that had any sick with divers diseases brought them unto him; and he laid his hands on every one of them and healed them."† Was there ever anything more delightful? The westering sun just disappearing behind the mountain, was reddening with its softest radiance the surface of the Galilean lake; and the sick ones of Capernaum were carried to His feet, while their bearers united with them in their pleadings for His help, and—no niggard He in the dispensation of His bless-

---
* John v. 28, 29.   † Luke iv. 40.

ings—He healed them all. But as I gaze on, the vision widens from Capernaum to a world, and still I see the blessed Redeemer exercising His divine and chosen vocation as the Healer of Humanity. They bring to Him "from every clime and coast" the sin-sick sons of Adam—the guilty, the backsliding, the burdened, the bereaved, the sorrowful, the forlorn, the tempted, the weary, the perplexed—and "he lays his hands on every one of them and heals them." What a hope is here for this sin-blasted earth! and what a work is that, beloved young brethren, to which you are called—the bringing of the burdened to the feet of Jesus? Realize, I pray you, the grandeur and nobleness of your mission; and as you go forth to your several spheres, carry this with you as the exposition and inspiration of your ministry: "He that believeth on me, the works that I do shall he do also; and greater works than these shall he do, because I go unto my Father."*

---

* John xiv. 12.

APPENDIX.

APPENDIX.

NOTE A.—Page 22.
THE LOGIC OF HUXLEY.

IN connection with the atheistic form of the evolution theory, I venture to reproduce here a letter to the New York *Tribune* on Huxley's Lectures, which were delivered in New York four years ago. I have been frequently asked for copies of the letter, and have been assured that its reissue in this permanent form will be welcomed by many. I have made only one or two verbal changes, leaving the argument as it originally stood.

To the Editor of The Tribune:

SIR:—Will you grant me a portion of your space for an examination of the logic of Prof. Huxley as that comes out in the lectures recently delivered by him in this city? As a layman in science I might have some delicacy in venturing into that domain which he and his coadjutors have made peculiarly their own, but logic is the same in its application to every department of inquiry, and a fallacy or an assumption in the reasoning of a man of science may be detected and exposed by one who is obliged, as I am, to take on trust the facts on which the argument is alleged to be founded.

Let it be understood, then, that I have no fault to find with Mr. Huxley as a discoverer of facts or as an exponent of comparative anatomy. In both of these respects he is beyond all praise of mine, and I am ready to sit at his feet; but when he begins to reason from the facts which he sets forth, then, like every other reasoner, he is amenable to the laws of argumentation, and his conclusions are to be tested by the relation which they bear to the premises which he has advanced, and by the proof which he furnishes for the premises themselves.

Let me say, also, that I have no prejudice against evolution, if that shall ever be fairly and fully established. I believe that it may be held in harmony with theism, and with a sincere acceptance of the Word of God. I am a disciple of one who has taught me in all things, and at every hazard, to follow truth; and the Gospel which I believe and preach leads me to say, with John Locke, that I am "more concerned to quit and renounce any opinion of my own, than oppose that of another, when truth appears against it; for 'tis truth alone I seek, and that will always be welcome to me, when or whencesoever it comes." But then it must be clearly proved to be the truth, and it is in the proof that Prof. Huxley has advanced that the weakness of his case appears.

His reasonings are mainly contained in his third lecture, but before proceeding to consider them it may be convenient to offer one or two strictures on some statements made by him in the first and second. He begins with enumerating three hypotheses regarding the order of nature. These are: The eternity of things as they are; the Miltonic theory, or the creation of the world in six natural days; and the theory of evolution, which finds in a gelatinous mass the common foundation of all life. These, he says, "so far as he knows, are the only three views." He does not allege, in so many words, that they are the only possible theories on the subject; but he reasons as if they were, and evidently wishes us to conclude that the elimination of the former two establishes the third. But as the force of a dilemma is destroyed when a third alternative, equally explanatory of the facts, is advanced, so the conclusiveness of a *tri*-lemma is nullified when a fourth hypothesis equally adapted to meet the case is set forth. Now there are many among us who cannot accept any one of the three hypotheses which he has suggested, but believe in creation in series; and there are others who are almost prepared to accept evolution, provided it be put forth as an explanation of the mode in which a presiding intelligence has brought things as they are into existence. This being the case, his classification is defective, and the force which his first lecture was designed to have, in the way of clearing the ground of everything but evolution, is completely neutralized.

But besides this logical blemish, I have to complain of a very unphilosophical bias which everywhere appears in his treatment of the idea of creation. He seems to be studiously fair, and we are apt to be imposed upon by the show of candor which he affects, until we go beneath the surface, when we perceive that beneath the veil of fair-sounding words he hides the most cynical of sneers. Thus he says: "Though we are quite clear about the constancy of nature at the present time and in the present order of things, it by no means follows necessarily that we are justified in expanding this generalization into the past, and in denying absolutely that there may have been a time when events did not follow a fixed order, *when the relations of cause and effect were not fixed and definite, and when external agencies did not intervene in the general order of nature. Cautious men will admit that such a change in the order of nature may have been possible, just as every candid thinker will admit that there may be a world in which two and two do not make four, and in which two straight lines do inclose a space.*" Now it is difficult to characterize this language without using stronger words than courtesy might sanction. But what are we to say when a man claiming to be a philosopher affirms (no, not affirms for if he had said it out plainly we should have had more respect for him, but let me say rather, insinuates) that to allege that the universe was created is virtually to declare that there was a time "when the relations of cause and effect were not fixed and definite"—as if there could be any more definite relation as cause and effect than that between the creator and the creature! And what are we to think when it is implied that to believe in creation is as absurd as to believe that there is a world where "two and two do not make four, and where two straight lines inclose a space?" Every one must see that such a world is an impossibility, for if two and two anywhere can make something different from four, then two must mean something different in such a place from its meaning here, or the whole science of numbers here rests on a foundation of sand. To say that creation may be possible, as that is possible, is only to assert its impossibility in the most offensive way. Yet all this is slipped out in the most innocent-looking way, as if he were making a very generous concession to the creationists, whereas, as we have seen, it is a most insulting denial of the very possibility of their theory, and that, too, without one word of offered proof, and under color of its being the utterance of a cautious man and a candid thinker.

Again, in vindicating himself for taking Milton's account of the creation, as an exposition of that usually held, he affirms that "*it is not his business to say what the Hebrew text contains and what it does not*," and after referring to the opinion of those who hold that the days of the creation in Genesis were not days of twenty-four hours each, but periods, he says "*a person who is not a Hebrew scholar can only stand by and admire the marvellous flexibility of a language which admits of such diverse interpretations.*" But the professor does not need to be a Hebrew scholar in order to be familiar with such "marvellous flexibility" of language. He knows that we have the very same "diverse interpretations" of the word "day" in English, for if I should say to him that the day has gone by when a foolish sneer can be accepted as a forcible argument, he would understand at once that I was not speaking of any such definite period as twenty-four hours. These are expressions quite unworthy of a man who makes such professions of impartiality, and they lead us to be most suspicious of his language, at the very moment when he is most humbly declaring that he is incompetent to form a judgment.

His second lecture is out of its proper place. In logical order it ought to have come last. It is not a proof, or a preparation for a proof, but rather a sort of alleged corroboration of a proof which is to be afterward furnished. Its only purpose, like that of Iago's rehearsal of Cassio's dream, is to

APPENDIX.—NOTE A. 237

" help to thicken other proofs which do demonstrate thinly." But had it come after the demonstration so-called it would have been received as an indication of the consciousness on the professor's own part that his demonstration was not convincing after all, and so it is dexterously employed as a kind of pioneer to prepare the way. There are in it the same characteristics as in the first. He is constantly seeming to make admissions which are found at length to be no admissions at all. He allows that the forms of species are persistent, and that there is little or nothing in the geologic records that sustains his position ; but he assumes that there are defects in these records, and then on the top of that assumes again that in these gaps the missing links in the process of evolution will be found. He will not hear of any *lacuna* between the first and second verses of Genesis, and when the theologian intimates that between the " beginning " of the one and the " chaos " of the other, there may have been an interval long enough for all the requirements of geology, he " stands by and admires " the flexibility of interpretations of which the Scriptures are capable. But it is time that we proceeded to the consideration of the much-heralded demonstration of evolution to which his third lecture was devoted.

And here any one accustomed to reasoning cannot fail to be struck with the loose and, indeed, misleading way in which he employs the term " demonstration." As defined by Webster, that word means, in its logical sense, " the act of proving by the syllogistic process, or the proof itself ;" and in its mathematical, " a course of reasoning showing that a certain result is a necessary consequence of assumed premises, these premises being definitions, axioms, and previously established propositions." Now it is a little difficult to determine in which of these two senses Huxley uses the word, but from his reference to the Copernican astronomy, which depends on the exactest mathematical calculations, it is evident that, in his conclusion at least, he means us to take it in its mathematical sense. But in his former lectures he employs it simply in its logical sense, as signifying proof—or that which is put forth as proof. He distinguishes between the evidence of testimony and the evidence of circumstance, and tells us that he has to do only with the latter. But circumstantial evidence never can amount to a demonstration unless, indeed, we are content to use that word as Huxley has done in the concluding sentence of his first lecture, when he says: "*I shall endeavor to show that there is a third kind of evidence, which, being as complete as any evidence which we can hope to obtain on such a subject, and being wholly and entirely in favor of evolution, may fairly be called demonstrative evidence of its having occurred.*" That is to say, when we have as much evidence as we can hope to obtain on any subject, provided it be in favor of our theory regarding it, we may call it demonstration ! A very comfortable canon surely, for by it we may demonstrate a great many other things than evolution.

But, as everybody knows, it is not enough, in order to prove a case from circumstantial evidence, that whatever evidence we have be in favor of our theory; it is required also that no other hypothesis can account for the circumstances. I have been furnished by a distinguished legal friend with a statement of the principles which regulate the value of circumstantial evidence, which may be thus condensed : " The process of proof by circumstantial evidence consists in reasoning from such facts as are *known* or *proved*, and thence establishing such as are conjectured to exist. The process is fatally vicious ; first, if any material circumstance from which we seek to deduce the conclusion depends itself on conjecture ; and, second, if the known facts are not such as to exclude to a reasonable degree of certainty every other hypothesis."

Now, tried by these two tests, the professor's argument is a failure. For, to take the latter first, after setting forth the horses of his new apocalypse, in order, and showing the gradual ascent of one above the other, in the two respects which he so minutely specifies, he makes no attempt to *prove* that the existence of these fossils is inconsistent with every other theory save that of evolution. He only *says*, in the naïvest possible manner: " The only other hypothesis that could be framed would be this, that the anchitherium,

APPENDIX.—NOTE A. 239

the hipparion, and the horse had been created separately and at separate epochs of time, *and for that there could be no scientific evidence.*" But where is the evidence, scientific or otherwise, that there was evolution? We see these fossils. Huxley *says* that they are as they are because the higher evolved itself out of the lower; we *say* that they are as they are because God created them in series; and for our belief in creation we have all the reasons, personal, philosophic, and historical, which we have for receiving the Bible as the Word of God. That may not be what Prof. Huxley would call scientific evidence, but, such as it is, it is better than no evidence at all, and Prof. Huxley gives us none.

For his argument rests on a conjecture, and so it violates the first of the two canons regulating circumstantial evidence. His conclusion is thus a hypothesis evolved from a hypothesis. To see that this is indeed the case, let us put his argument in syllogistic form. It is as follows: Wherever we have an ascending series of animals with modifications of structure rising one above another, the later forms must have evolved themselves from the earlier. In the case of these fossil horses we have such a series, therefore the theory of evolution is established universally for all organized and animal life. Now even if we admit his premises, every one must see that the conclusion is far too sweeping. It ought to have been confined to the horses of which he was treating. But passing that, let us ask where is the proof of the major premise? Indeed that premise is suppressed altogether, and he nowhere attempts to show that the existence of an ascending series of animals, with modifications of structure rising one above another, is *an infallible indication* that the higher members of the series evolved themselves out of the lower. There, in the suppressed premise, in which Whately cautions us to look most warily after fallacy, the flaw in Huxley's reasoning is to be found. He has taken for granted in the major premise of his argument, which is conveniently out of sight, the very thing which, amid a great flourish of trumpets, he set out to demonstrate. Nobody denies the existence of the fossil horses, but his inference from their existence, to the effect that the later horse is an evolution of the earlier anchitherium, is purely and entirely begged. The existence of a series does not necessarily involve the evolution of the higher members of it from the lower. The steps of a stair rise up one above another, but we cannot reason that therefore the whole staircase has developed itself out of the lowest step. It may be possible to arrange all the different modifications of the steam-engine, from its first and crudest form up to its latest and most completely organized structure, in regular gradation; but that would not prove that the last grew out of the first. No doubt in such a case there has been progress—no doubt there has been development too—but it was progress guided and development directed *by a presiding and intervening mind.* And nowhere in all the existing order of things will you find modifications increasing and perpetuating themselves except under the intervention of some intelligent mind. Therefore all present experience is against this major premise which Huxley has so quietly taken for granted. It is a pure conjecture. I will go so far as to say that even if he should find in the geologic records all the intervening forms he desires, these will not furnish evidence that the higher members of the series rose out of the lower by a process of evolution. The existence of a graduated series is one thing; the growth of the series out of its lowest member is quite another. No doubt if it could be proved that there was such a growth, we should certainly find such a series; but it is a mistake to suppose that, because of that, the existence of the series has proved that there was a growth. This being the case, the argument of Huxley is something very different from a demonstration—to wit, a fallacy.

 Indeed, to affirm, as he did, that evolution stands exactly on the same basis as the Copernican theory of the motions of the heavenly bodies, is an assertion so astounding that we can only "stand by and admire" the "marvellous" effrontery with which it was made. That theory rests on facts presently occurring before our eyes, investigated and reasoned from with strictest mathematical precision. It is not an inference made by somebody, from a record of facts existing in far-off and prehistoric, possibly also prehuman, ages. It is verified every day by occurrences that happen according to its laws. But where do we see evolution going on to-day? If evolution rests on a basis as sure as astronomy, why do we not see one species passing into another now, even as we see the motions of the planets through the heavens? Why cannot its votaries foretell that at a certain time, and in a certain place, not too far for personal inspection by us, some modification in the structure of an animal or a plant shall occur, without any human intervention, even as atronomers predict the occurrence of a transit of Venus across the sun?

We know that astronomy is true, because we are verifying its conclusions every day of our lives, on land and on sea. We set our clocks according to its conclusions, and navigate our ships in accordance with its predictions; but where have we anything approaching even infinitesimally to this, with evolution? It may be that there is truth in it; and whenever that shall be made clear to us, we are ready to accept it. But, with Prof. Huxley himself, "*we have an awkward habit—no, I won't call it that, for it is a valuable habit—of reasoning, so that we believe nothing unless there is evidence for it, and we have a way of looking upon belief which is not based on evidence, not only as illogical, but immoral.*" The professor is welcome to the application of his own principle. For me, the demonstration of Huxley, so far as it has been set before us here, is of the same sort as the conjecture of Topsy, "'spects I growed." It is after all, despite the words he has multiplied around it, the "'spects" of Huxley. As such it is worthy of respect—just as any opinion or conjecture of such a man must have a certain degree of importance—but as a demonstration it is an imposition, which we have done our best to nail to the counter, that it may not get into currency.

I am, yours faithfully,

WM. M. TAYLOR.

NEW YORK, *Oct.* 11, 1876.

NOTE B.—Page 23.

The essay of Dr. Mozley, from which the citations in the Lecture are taken, is the most Butlerian piece of reasoning which the present century has produced. We quote here the whole passage from which our extracts are taken, in the hope that our readers may be induced to study the essay as a whole:

"We know Mr. Darwin's own account of natural selection; and from this very account it allows that natural selection is not an agent at all, but a result. It is the effect which proceeds from a favorable modification or development of structure in one animal in the struggle for existence with another animal not thus additionally endowed; viz, his survivorship and continuance on the field while the other perishes. There is an unknown reservoir and spring of productiveness in nature; and some improvement or augmentation is supposed to have come out of it, and some animal to have been the recipient of it; this is the *productive* agency in the case. This productive agency having operated, then there is a result, in the particular condition of scarcity of food under which animal life labors, which proceeds from it, which result is the preservation of one animal and the death of another, or natural selection. Natural selection, then, is not an agent, but a result; and it is moreover only a negative or privitive result.

"The favored party in this struggle, the party that lives, would have lived all the same had there been no struggle for existence, and no natural selection; and he does not owe his existence and continuance to natural selection; he only owes his *sole* existence to it, as distinguished from the fate of a rival who perishes. The difference, therefore, which natural selection makes is not that one of these animals is preserved, but that the other is destroyed, and that is the one sole result in natural selection. Had the supply of food in the world been infinite and inexhaustible, both of these animals would have lived, for both would have had enough to live upon; but the supply being limited, one of them dies. Natural selection, then, has nothing to do with the creation of any favorable addition to Nature; it is only the removal of those who do not possess the addition. They perish, and the scene of creation thus becomes a very different one from what it would have been had there been no natural selection. Could we suppose an innumerable and inexhaustible supply of nutriment in the world, and consequently no struggle for existence, the area of Nature would have been a crowded field of irregular as well as regular forms of animal life; all those wide interstices which now separate species from species would have been filled up, and the earth would have teemed with a chaotic rabble of animal structures, lower forms and higher, perfect species and imperfect; the ascents of Nature being almost merged and lost in the gradational multitude; all would have survived because there was food for all. Natural selection clears this ground, interposes intervals, and arranges Nature into groups and masses. But it does this work, not as an agent, but only as an effect—the destructive effect of the scarcity of food. Without the struggle for existence regular forms would not have monopolized the ground—Nature would not have been seen upon the unencumbered pedestal on which she is now, or presented her present structural appearance. But natural selection only weeds, and does not plant; it is the drain of Nature carrying off the irregularities, the monstrosities, the abortions; it comes in after and upon the active developments of Nature to prune and thin them; but it does not create a species, it does not possess one productive or generative function.

"Natural selection figures in language, indeed, as an active and creative power. It 'effects improvement;' it 'checks deviations;' it 'develops structure;' it has 'accumulative action;' it 'works silently and insensibly wherever opportunity offers;' it has made, indeed, every organ and limb of every existing animal. The species are its workmanship; they come out of the hands of this great artificer, who is described as fashioning the clay of life. Natural selection is not only an agent; it is even a designing agent; it 'acts for the good of each creature;' it is 'always trying to economize;' it has always an object before it and acts with an aim. But all this is only the phraseology of metaphor, summing up and condensing consequences under the figure and impersonation of a cause. We meet an effect under the form of a cause, as we meet our own figure in a shop mirror in the street departing from the very place at which we are going to arrive. Upon this very account natural selection designs perfectly, because it is, in fact, itself the successful result; it always hits, because the aimer is, in truth, the mark; its intention is only metamorphosed fact. We have to carry on this interpretation of the action and design of natural selection as we read Mr. Darwin; and though we by no means grudge him the liberty of metaphor, we are sometimes conscious of an exegetical task in extracting the real fact out of the language of figure. Natural selection is superior to human selection. What does this mean? That one is a better exercise of choice than the other? No; it means that whereas human selection is choice, trial, and experiment, and may, therefore, fail, natural selection is secure because it is the favorable result to begin with. In human selection the choice aims at the event; in natural selection the event makes the choice. Natural selection endows the woodpecker with its instrument—'a striking instance of adaptation'—*i. e.*, it does not give *one* woodpecker its instrument; it has nothing to do with that; it only kills off another woodpecker that has not got it. Natural selection forms the flying squirrel with its parachute; *i. e.*, it makes away with another squirrel who has not got a parachute and is at a disadvantage in the locality. Natural selection has 'reduced the wings' of some species of beetles in Madeira. That means that those species which *had* reduced or shortened wings were naturally selected or survived, whereas others with full wings, by reason of this very completeness of them, perished, because they flew, and, flying, flew over the sea, and, flying over the sea, got carried away by winds, and could not get back again to land. We have thus to commute the language of natural selection as fast as we receive it; to drive metaphorically forward and really backward at the same time, and at every moment to transpose, by an understanding and arrangement with ourselves, the cart before the horse, into the natural order of the horse first."—*Essays Historical and Theological, by J. B. Mozley, D.D., Vol. II.*, pp. 396-399.

NOTE C.—PAGE 161.

In reference to the Gospel by Matthew, we take the liberty of quoting here a section from a little volume by a valued personal friend, in which the whole argument is compressed into the briefest space :

" We affirm that the canonical Gospel of St. Matthew could not be the 'obscure and popular elaboration' of a multitude of writers, or be the result of an intermixture, accomplished in equally casual and multitudinous manner, of two familiar documents, and other popular traditions, because there is a unity of *style* in the whole Gospel, which imprints on every part of it the individual stamp of its author—which reveals itself in charateristic idioms and in favorite turns of expression, shot like finest threads inextricably throughout the entire web of the Gospel, giving a specific and plainly featured character, an inalienable identity, not only to the Gospel as a whole, but to every section of it equally. The discourses and the narratives are written in the same hand. The first two chapters, whose authenticity is sometimes disputed, bear the impress of the same literary mould as the other chapters of the Gospel : so that M. Renan's theory could only be accepted on condition of the astounding miracle, that every one of the thousands who in divers times and places added the sentences and paragraphs, from St. Mark or elsewhere, which make up the present compost, either possessed congenitally the precise mental habitudes and linguistic peculiarities of the writer of the Logia, or they were supernaturally endowed with St. Matthew's most original and almost eccentric style, whenever they lifted a pen to insert a word into the original document of the Logia which they possessed. This argument is not vapid rodomontade, as it would be if we did not exhibit the minute subtle idiomatic harmonies and larger expressional forms which pervade this Gospel, interlacing it into an organic unity by a network as fine and strong as the nervous tissues of a living body.

"The number and continuity of our examples place our argument beyond the reach of cavil. We the more willingly reproduce this argument in something like its full force, because we are acquainted with no English work in which it is at all adequately exhibited, though Westcott, Norton, Roberts ('Discussions of the Gospels'), and most of our commentators, present fragments of the evidence. We are largely indebted to Gersdorf's invaluable work, 'Beitrage zur Sprachcharacteristik der Schriftsteller des N. T.' (Leipzig, 1816), for most of the illustrations we array as evidence to prove that St. Matthew's Gospel—as we have it—was indubitably written by one person :

"'1. The peculiar idiomatic form of expression seen in Matt. i. 20 : Ταῦτα δὲ αὐτοῦ ἐνθυμηθέντος, ἰδοῦ, occurs nine times at least : —ii. 1 ; ii. 13 ; ii. 19 ; ix. 18 ; ix. 32 ; xii. 46 ; xvii. 5 ; xxvi. 47 ; xxviii. 5. The word ἰδοῦ occurs often in the New Testament; but only in one other passage does it follow the genitive absolute. It occurs in Matthew fifty-three times. There is a similar peculiarity of construction in the use of ἰδοῦ, which occurs nowhere else in the New Testament. It is seen in ii. 9 : Οἱ δὲ, ἀκούσαντες τοῦ βασιλέως, ἐπορεύθησαν· καὶ ἰδοῦ. For this use of καὶ ἰδοῦ, after the nominative participle, cf. viii. 32-34 ; xxvi. 50, 51 ; xxviii. 8, 9, 19, 20 ; cf. also, iii. 16, 17 ; ix. 1, 2, 19, 20 ; xii. 9, 10 ; xv. 21, 22 ; xix. 15, 16 ; xxvii. 50, 51. There is still another construction of καὶ ἰδοῦ, which is proper to this Gospel, and found nowhere else in the New Testament, in which it follows the dative participle : Καὶ ἐμβάντι αὐτῷ—ἠκολούθησαν—αἱ ἰδοῦ: viii. 23, 24, 28, 29 ; xxviii. 1.

"'2. In the first Gospel the adverb οὕτως is always placed before the verb : οὕτως ἦν : i. 18 ; ii. 5 ; iii. 15 ; v. 12, 16 ; vi. 9, 30 ; etc., etc. In the other Gospels it is placed sometimes before, sometimes after.

"'3. There is a very frequent form in Matthew, μάγοι παρεγένοντο λέγοντες : ii. 1 ; cf. ii. 20 ; iii. 1 ; iii. 17 ; viii. 5 ; ix. 18 ; xiii. 36 ; xiv. 15, etc., etc. Now Luke and Mark, on the contrary, always add αὐτῷ or αὐτοῖς.

"'4. This style of phrase, καὶ πέμψας, εἶπε, cf. xi. 2, 3; xiv. 10; xxii. 7, and πορευθέντες μάθετε, ix. 13; xi. 4; xvii. 27; xxi. 6; xxii. 15, etc., etc., is quite characteristic of Matthew. The first occurs nowhere else in the Gospels, and the second very rarely in Luke, and but once in Mark. (It may be observed, indeed, that there are more of these nice points of agreement between Matthew and Luke than between Matthew and Mark, which are yet supposed to be only different mixtures of the same elements).

"'5. Διεγερθεὶς ἀπὸ τοῦ ὕπνου, i. 24; cf. xiv. 2; xxvii. 64; xxviii. 7. All the other writers of the New Testament use the preposition ἐκ with this verb. The expression, κατ' ὄναρ, is equally peculiar to this Gospel.

"'6. The adverb τότε occurs ninety times in the Gospel of Matthew. It occurs only six times in Mark, and fourteen times in Luke. Σφόδρα is very frequent in the first Gospel, and is always placed after the verb. It occurs only once in Mark (xvi. 4) and once in Luke (xviii. 23).

"'7. Ἀνεχώρησαν occurs once in Mark (iii. 7) with the preposition πρός. Luke never uses it. It appears ten times in Matthew, and always with the preposition εἰς.

"'We have not nearly ended this catalogue, but must stop. The phrase ἡ βασίλεια τῶν οὐρανῶν is repeated thirty-two times throughout every section of this Gospel, in discourses and narratives alike. It appears nowhere in Mark or Luke. In Matthew the peculiar idiom, ἵνα πληρωθῇ τὸ ῥηθὲν, or, τοῦτο ὅλον δὲ γέγονεν ἵνα, proclaims the application and fulfilment of a prophetic passage, but only in this Gospel. Many other words and phrases, such as ὁ πονηρός, συντέλεια τοῦ αἰῶνος, συμβούλιον λαμβάνειν, μαθητεύειν, are peculiar to Matthew, and occur several times in different parts of his Gospel. And the expression, υἱὸς Δαβίδ, is likewise characteristic of it, occurring in i. 20; ix. 27; xii. 23; xv. 22; xx. 30, 31, etc.; occurring accordingly in all parts of it, whilst it occurs but rarely in Mark and Luke.

"'As corroborative evidence, we remark, the Latinized forms occurring in this Gospel, such as κοδράντην (v. 26), for the Latin *quadrans*, φραγελλόω, for Latin *flagello* (xxvii. 26), etc., indicate one hand in the composition of the Gospel; and, further, that it came from the hand of Matthew. " When," as Dr. Davidson says (" Introduction to the New Testament," i., 56), " it is remembered that Matthew, as a tax-gatherer for the Roman government, must have come into contact, by the very nature of his office, with persons using the Latin language, these Latinisms are accounted for." '"—*A Review of the Vie de Jesus of M. Renan, by J. B. Paton, M.A., Principal of Nottingham Training Institute, England*, pp. 95-58.

NOTE D.—PAGE 212.

Not until after this Lecture was written could I lay my hands on Canon Westcott's little work entitled " Characteristics of the Gospel Miracles," in which with his accustomed thoroughness that excellent scholar views the miracles of Christ, as in themselves an Epiphany, classifying them under the heads of Miracles of Power, Miracles of Providence, Miracles of Healing, and Miracles on the Spirit World. Before attempting to deal with this department of the subject, I sought with great diligence for Dr. Westcott's volume, but was everywhere met with the answer, " out of print ;" and now that I have had the opportunity of examining it, I find, to my great satisfaction, that I have been led for myself into some trains of thought quite similar to those which he pursues. Such a book should not, surely, be suffered to become inaccessible to the students of to-day, and a new edition of it would be a great boon.

NOTE E.—PAGE 218.

In this connection what Westcott, in the work referred to in the last note, says in regard to the miracles of healing is equally applicable to these miracles, as he calls them, of providence. " They are presented to us as a revelation of hope, of restoration, of forgiveness ; of hope, as wrought in an age of signal distress ; of restoration, in the universality of their extent ; of forgiveness, in the spiritual antetypes of their working. And if we take this larger view of their essential nature, I do not see how we can conceive of a Divine Saviour without such deeds of love. A gospel without miracles would be, if I may use the image, like a church without sacraments. The outward pledge of the spiritual gift would be wanting. Teaching and example would remain, but faith would find no way opened to 'the world to come.' "—*Characteristics of the Gospel Miracles*, pp. 43, 44.

www.ingramcontent.com/pod-product-compliance
Lightning Source LLC
Chambersburg PA
CBHW021410230426
43666CB00006B/702